SOUTH AMERICAN

KINSHIP

EIGHT KINSHIP SYSTEMS
FROM BRAZIL AND COLOMBIA

INTERNATIONAL MUSEUM OF CULTURES

PUBLICATION 18

WILLIAM R. MERRIFIELD
Series Editor

DESMOND C. DERBYSHIRE
General Editor
Academic Publications Coordinator

SOUTH AMERICAN

KINSHIP

EIGHT KINSHIP SYSTEMS
FROM BRAZIL AND COLOMBIA

William R. Merrifield
editor

THE INTERNATIONAL MUSEUM OF CULTURES

Dallas, Texas

1985

© 1985 by the Summer Institute of Linguistics, Inc.

Library of Congress Catalog
Card No: 85-080410

ISBN: 0-88312-173-5

ISSN: 0079-7669

Reprinted 1987

This title is available at:

THE INTERNATIONAL MUSEUM OF CULTURES
7500 W. Camp Wisdom Road
Dallas, TX 75236

TABLE OF CONTENTS

PREFACE

The eight studies of this volume, from Brazil and
Colombia, result from the investigations of SIL field
linguists whose primary research relates to questions
of theoretical linguistics and linguistic applications
in the areas of literacy and translation. Such research, particularly in these applied areas, must take
into account its cultural context if it is to be
accounted relevant. Such research, as a matter of
fact, may not even be possible without adequate attention to cultural matters. This is as it should be
since the culture of every human group is important
and must be respected.

The languages represented by these studies per-
tain to five language families. Paumarí is Arawakan,
Cogui is Chibchan, Guahibo is Guahiban, three of the
languages (Coreguaje, Cubeo, and Tucano) are Tucanoan,
and two languages (Kayabí and Suruí) are Tupian. All
but Cogui are spoken by peoples of lowland (Amazonian)
South America, and all the communities which speak
them are organized primarily around the family, on the
basis of kinship. An understanding of kinship within
these communities is, thus, the sine qua non of
'taking into account' the cultural context of the
linguistic research being carried on there.

While the study of family and kinship can be a
very large one to undertake, the analysis of a system
of kinship terminology provides both a manageable
starting point and an important foundation stone for
understanding the larger social organization of small-
scale communities of this sort. It is, moreover, an
ideal contribution for a linguist to make to the
anthropological study of a community because terminological systems are, after all, linguistic systems.

Several of the papers in this volume limit themselves to the analysis of a kinship terminology, with-

1

out much further detail about other social institutions. The Suruí paper is one of the exceptions in including a preliminary statement concerning residence and marriage. The Suruí kinship data are of particular interest because they describe a community which has only recently been available for study by westerners. The paper, which was first drafted in 1974, provided seminal ideas for Merrifield (1983), and describes bifurcate categories in a way which clarifies, I believe, the nature of similar systems previously described in the literature, such as the related Tupian Sirionó system of Bolivia described by Scheffler and Lounsbury (1971). The paper also begins to apply an insight by Simons (1983) from systemic linguistics which we believe enhances traditional approaches to componential analysis, reducing the arbitrariness in ranking conceptual dimensions by recognizing simultaneity as a possible type of dependency relation.

Gawthorne's description of Cogui kinship, while differing from all the others of the volume in treating a highland Chibchan language, is a useful addition of linguistic and cultural detail to the earlier description of this difficult-to-study society by Reichel-Dolmatoff (1950-51).

Gralow's Coreguaje data, from a Western Tucanoan language of Colombia, are of interest in defining bifurcate categories in the same manner as the Tupian Suruí and Sirionó of Brazil and Bolivia. At the same time, Coreguaje differs from these bilaterally symmetrical systems by displaying a classical Lounsbury (1964a) skewing rule of Omaha Type I. Gralow has done a good job of tracking down the extension of terms in the context of this rule.

Goehner and West have also provided excellent data from Tucano which show a strong agnatic bias like Coreguaje, but in this case tied directly to the patrisib membership of kinsmen rather than to an Omaha rule. Unlike Coreguaje, Tucano defines its bifurcate categories more on the order of Mayoruna (Fields and Merrifield 1980), a Panoan language of Peru and Brazil, and of Kariera of aboriginal Australia (Romney and Epling 1958).

Kondo's Guahibo data also reveal a system of bifurcate categories like Tucano, but without the agnatic biases of either Tucano or Coreguaje. Kondo builds on earlier descriptions of Guahibo kinship terms, adding and clarifying detail.

Morse documents still another Tucanoan system in Cubeo which defines bifurcate categories like Suruí, Sirionó, and Coreguaje, providing additional detail and clarification beyond that given by Goldman (1963) both on sibs and kinship terms.

Odmark and Landin, in addition to giving an analysis of the Paumarí kinship terminology, provide useful and interesting detail regarding marriage and residence among this culturally-depressed group. The kinship system is symmetrically bilateral and employs a Mayoruna-type definition of bifurcate categories.

The volume closes with a preliminary statement by Weiss concerning Kayabí kinship which, interestingly enough, points to an Iroquoian definition of bifurcate categories, not unlike that of Seneca (Lounsbury 1964b).

All eight articles of this volume take an extensionist view of kinship and make serious attempts to provide formal statements regarding the primary ranges of reference of terms as well as for their full extensions. It is hoped that these papers will contribute to the ongoing study of comparative kinship both in South America and elsewhere.

WILLIAM R. MERRIFIELD

Dallas, Texas
April, 1985

REFERENCES

Fields, Harriet L. and William R. Merrifield. 1980. Mayoruna (Panoan) kinship. Ethnology 19:1-28.

Goldman, Irving. 1963. The Cubeo: Indians of the Northwest Amazon. Urbana: University of Illinois Press.

Lounsbury, Floyd G. 1964a. A formal analysis of the Crow- and Omaha-type kinship terminologies. In W. H. Goodenough (ed.), Explorations in cultural anthropology, 351-93. New York: McGraw-Hill Book Co.

-----. 1964b. The structural analysis of kinship semantics. In H. G. Lunt (ed.), Proceedings of the ninth international congress of linguists, 1973-93. The Hague: Mouton and Co.

Merrifield, William R. 1983. On the formal analysis of kinship terminologies. In Fred Agard et al. (eds.), Essays in honor of Charles F. Hockett (=Cornell contributions to linguistics 5). Leiden: E. J. Brill. Pp. 371-404.

Reichel-Dolmatoff, Gerardo. 1950-51. Los Kogi: Una tribu de la Sierra Nevada de Santa Marta, Colombia. Bogotá: Revista del Instituto Etnológico.

Romney, A. Kimball & P. J. Epling. 1958. A simplified model of Kariera kinship. American anthropologist 60:59-74.

Scheffler, Harold W. and Floyd G. Lounsbury. 1971. A study in structural semantics: the Sirionó kinship system. Englewood Cliffs: Prentice-Hall, Inc.

Simons, Gary. 1983. Semantic reconstruction and change in the kinship systems of the Southeast Solomons. Paper presented at the 15th Pacific Science Congress, Dunedin, New Zealand.

ON SURUI (TUPIAN) SOCIAL ORGANIZATION

Carolyn Bontkes & William R. Merrifield
Summer Institute of Linguistics, Brazil & Dallas
1

This paper describes residence and marriage patterns among the Suruí, a Tupi-speaking people of southeastern Rondônia, Brazil, and presents a formal account of their kinship system. Residence is predominantly patrilocal and marriage is with a cross cousin or, preferably, a sister's daughter. This latter type of marriage is without doubt an important factor in having skewed an otherwise symmetrical Dravidian system of kinship terminology in such a way that father's sister is termed a classificatory grandmother, and certain cross kinsmen of the first ascending and first descending generations are classed with cross cousins. The paper is of particular interest in that it represents the situation of a Tupian people who, at the time of data collection, had been in extensive contact with the outside world for less than five years.

The first peaceful contact in recent times was made with the Suruí in June of 1969 at the Brazilian government Post 'Sete de Setembro'.2 By late 1974, 150 persons had settled at the Post while a group of about sixty-five had settled fifty miles away in the Brazilian frontier town of Espigão d'Oeste. The marriage and residence practices of those at the post are here discussed briefly before considering the kinship terminology.

Figure 1 presents the arrangement of buildings at the Post as they existed in August, 1974. The government buildings and three small Suruí shelters (7,8,15) are located at the north end of the airstrip. The government buildings include kitchen (11), dormitories (5,6), administration/pharmacy (10), and a house for a Suruí family. Three buildings were under construction: kitchen (12), administration/pharmacy (13), and a house for a Suruí family (14). Three Suruí longhouses (2,3,4) and two small shelters (9,17) are located near the south end of the airstrip.

5

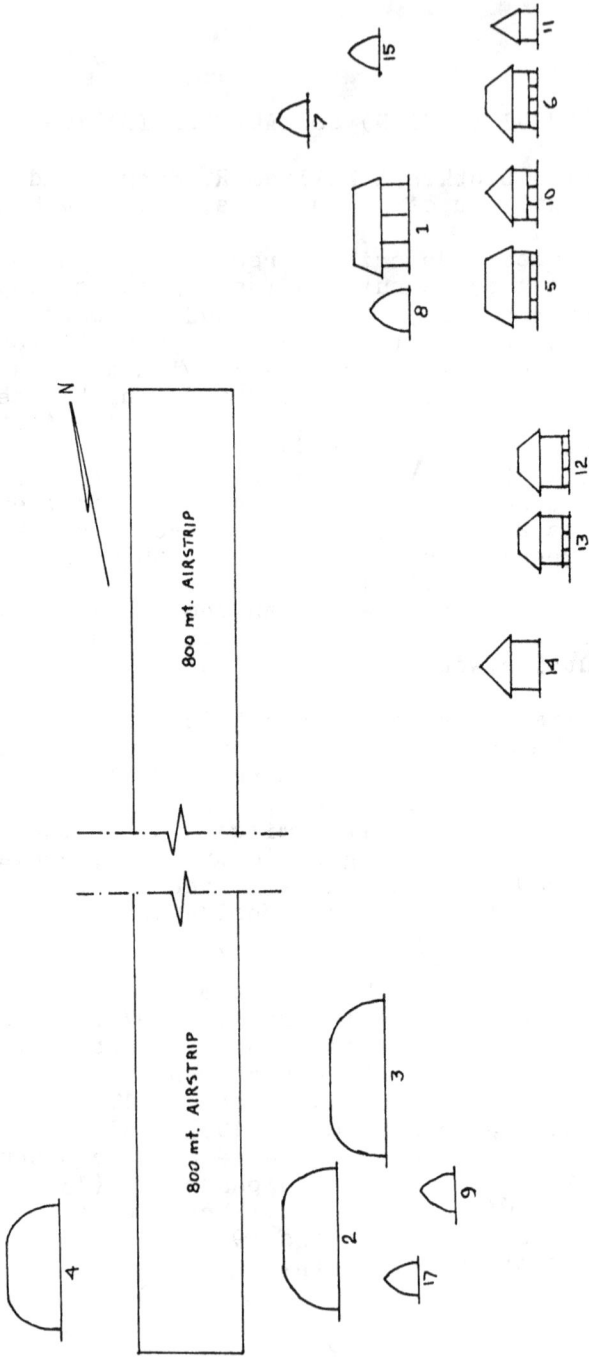

Figure 1. Arrangement of buildings, government Post "Sete de Setembro."

The government houses have shingle roofs and
walls of split palm. Most of the buildings have ele-
vated floors of split palm, the exception being the
kitchen (11) and house (1). The latter building has a
palm roof with no walls or floor, and is occupied by a
Surui family. The small shelters are of Surui manufac-
ture, made for mothers with new-born babies. Mother
and child live in these shelters for up to three
months. Other shelters may also be used by women in
menses, or by young girls engaged in puberty rites.
Such girls occupy the shelter with a young companion
for at least three months.

Surui longhouses are large, oval-shaped structures made of thin wood poles covered with palm leaves
except near the ground where a 'wall' about one meter
high is made of the outer bark of trees.

Shelter 8, originally built as a puberty house,
is now occupied by a Surui family consisting of a man,
his wife, and their three children. They moved into
this shelter because the man needed continuous medical
help. Shelter 7 is occupied by two mothers and their
new-born babies plus a young boy who is there to aid
the women. Shelter 9 is also occupied by a mother and
her new baby and a young boy. Shelters 15 and 17 are
made for women in menses and are only used for that
purpose. Dormitory 5 is occupied by young Surui men
and boys who have been working for the government on a
permanent basis and who no longer live with their
families.

Types of marriage

The preferred type of marriage among the Surui is
between a mother's brother and his sister's daughter
(real or classificatory). A man, therefore, tends to
have a close relationship with his sister, so that he
will be able to marry her daughter. It appears that
the oldest male sibling has priority to marry the
first available daughter.

Bilateral cross-cousin marriage is also acceptable. In this regard, it should be noted that marriage to the sister's daughter in two successive generations results in the sister's daughter also being
the matrilateral cross cousin, as can be seen in (1).

(1)

```
         ┌──────┬──────┐
         ┊      │      │
         f      ┊      │
         ┊      ┊      ┊
      ┌──┴──┬───┴──┐   ┊
      │     ┊      │   ┊
      ┊     f  =   m
      ┊          │
      m   =   f
     ego
```

Of seventy-eight marriages where the genealogical relationship was known in 1974, fifty-three were with the sister's daughter and twenty-five were with a cross cousin--twenty-one patrilateral and four matrilateral. A young man eligible to marry his father's sister's daughter may elope with her and stay hidden until her mother's brother (who would have priority) is no longer angry or has acquired another wife.3

Polygyny is also practiced, with the result that an older brother may have up to three wives while a younger brother has none. A girl marries immediately upon leaving the puberty house.

It is not acceptable to marry a sibling or parallel cousin, or kinswoman referred to as mother or grandmother. In one known case, however, a man claimed paternity of his father's wife's child, the wife being both a parallel cousin to his mother and his own paternal cross-cousin. It is not certain whether this is considered incest or whether it is acceptable because of the cross-cousin relationship.

In another case, a girl became pregnant by her classificatory grandson in 1979. She was given traditional medicine by her parents to cause an obortion since this was still very much taboo. It does seem, however, that these rules are loosening up a bit at present because of a lack of women for marriage. This is also resulting in some of the men marrying women from other language groups.

Residence patterns

The residence of individual Surui families is continually shifting. Nevertheless, Figures 2-5 provide typical locations of families and their hammock arrangements in longhouses as they existed at one time. These particular arrangements are no longer true at the time of writing, but the principles of arrangement remain the same. These principles may be enumerated as follows:

1. A group of brothers (real or classificatory), together with their wives and children, ideally form the core of a household. The brother with the largest family is usually the head.

2. The sisters of these brothers, with their husbands and children, including married children, are often also found in the household. Yámabúra (168, Figure 4) is the parent of Pangóxijodóm (94); Moykábea and Mamúgatòa (169,165) are the parents of the women (170,172). The parents have presumably moved in with their daughter's families because (1) the fathers have no living brothers, (2) they have no married sons of their own, and (3) their wives are classificatory sisters to the men of the household (199,200,201).

3. A widowed sister and her children are welcome because she provides daughters as wives for her brothers. She can also cook for any widowed or unmarried brother and his children.

4. A widowed sister-in-law and her children may marry another of the brothers or remain alone within the household. Whether or not she marries another of the brothers, they provide for her and their brother's children who are terminologically classified as their own. An illustration of this is Lakabáteru (192, Figure 3) whose husband died. She remained in the house for some time, but did not marry either of the other brothers (186,187) even though one (186) was a widower. Later, she traveled in another group with her own unmarried brother (340), but presumably would be welcome to move back to her old spot in the longhouse. Traveling with her own brother she is able to cook for him while he provides for her. She is also a potential provider of a wife for him through her daughters (193,194).

5. A wife's unmarried brother, or widowed brother and his children, may live in the household of his sister's husband and his brothers. This occurs especially when he has no brothers of his own with whom to organize a household, or when none of his brothers are

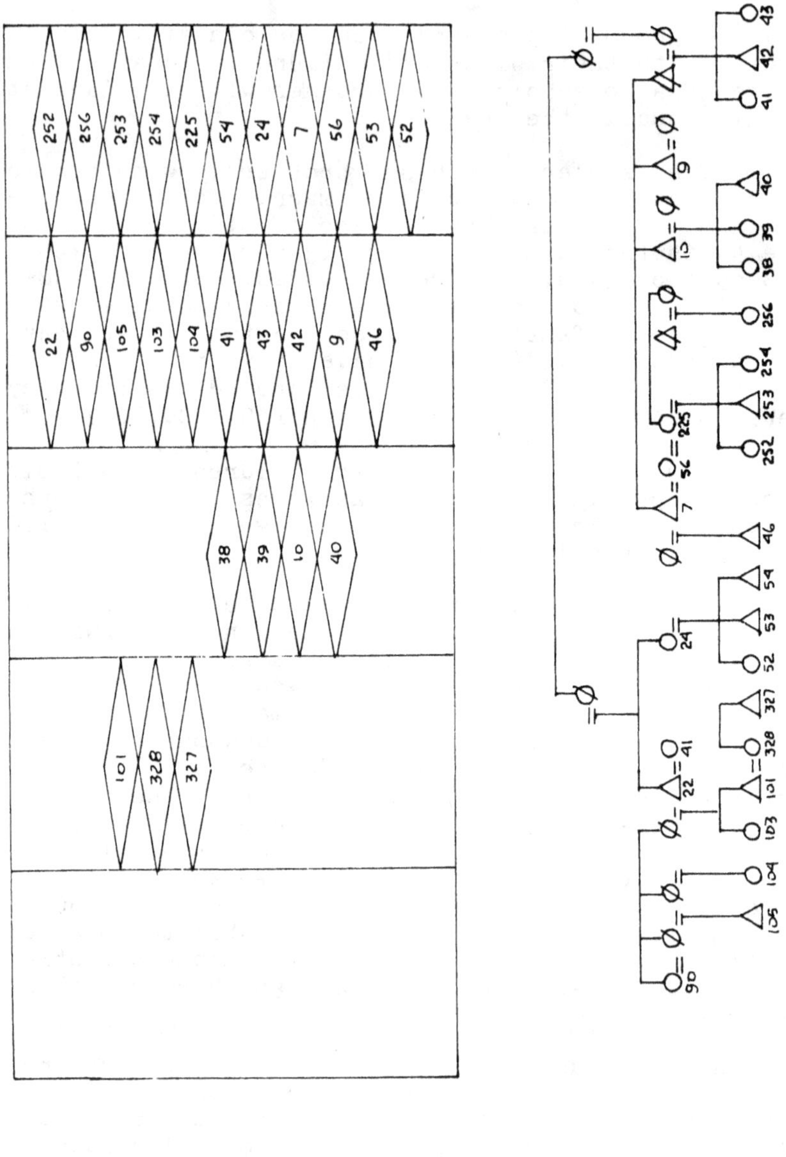

Figure 2. House 1.

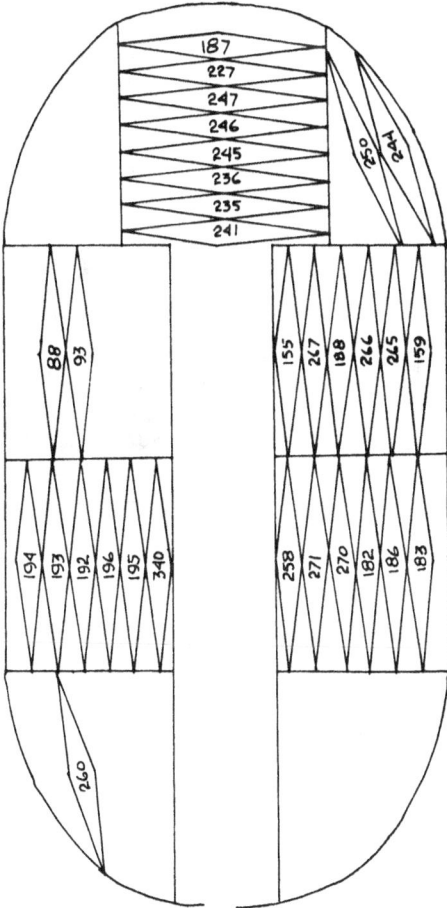

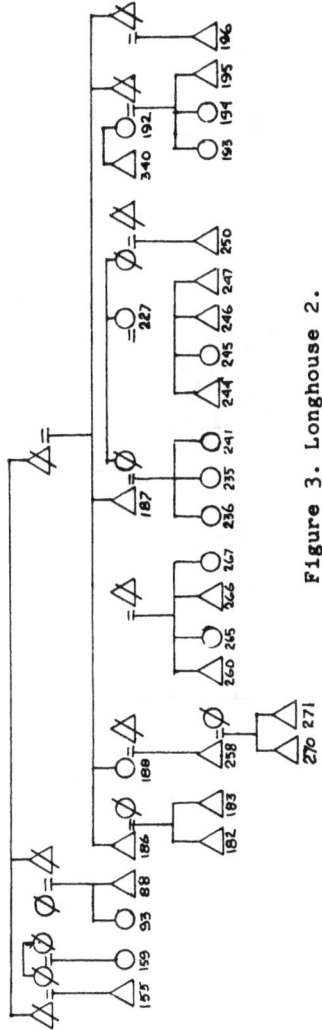

Figure 3. Longhouse 2.

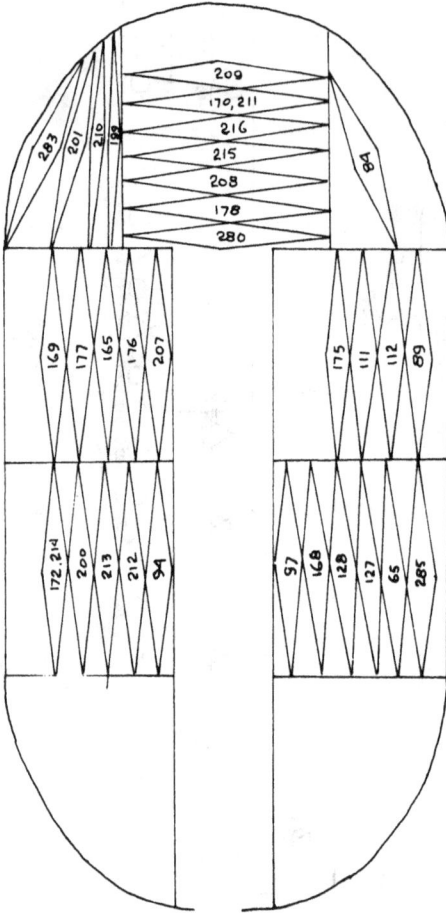

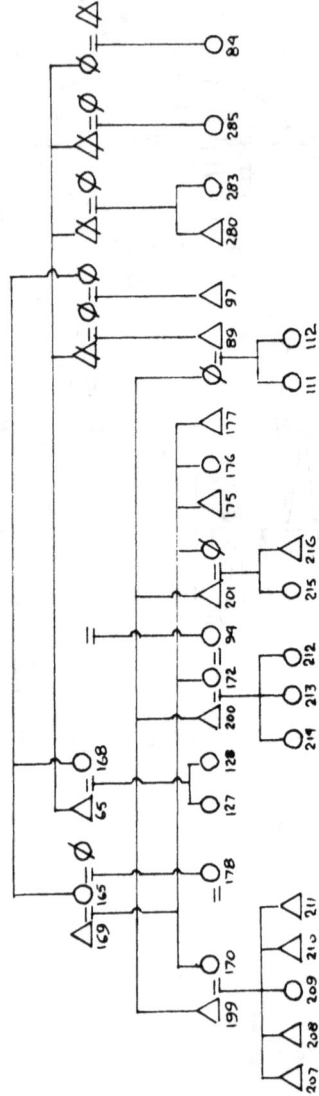

Figure 4. Longhouse 3.

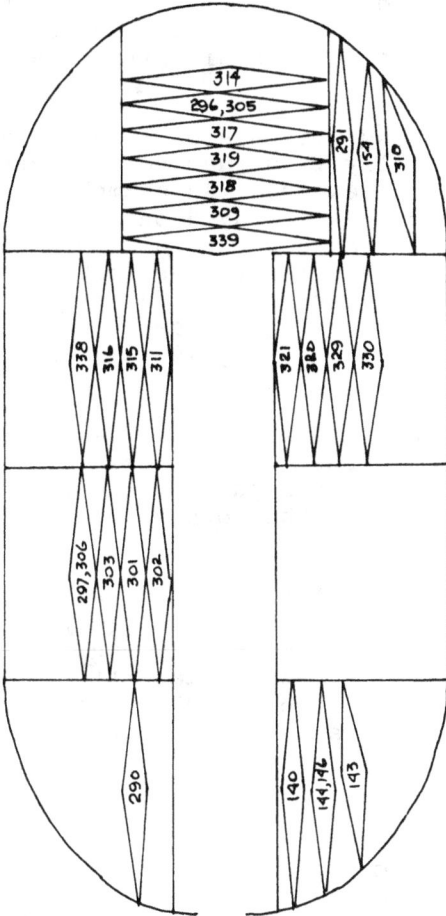

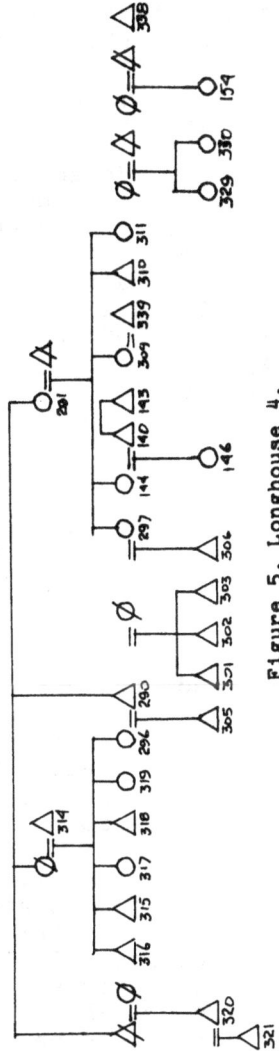

Figure 5. Longhouse 4.

married. His sister prepares his food and is a potential provider of a wife. He in turn hunts to provide
for his sister's family. He is welcomed by his sister's husband who may also be his mother's brother.
The mother's brother, among other things, tatoos the
permanent ceremonial markings on the faces of his
sororal nephews and nieces. Mámugpóya (22) lives part
of the time with his sister Xoyúb (24) in house 1
(Figure 2), and part of the time with his wife's (90)
extended family.

A widowed brother-in-law with his children may
remain in the house, especially if he has no brothers
with wives to cook for him elsewhere. An example of
this is Yámnér (314, Figure 5) who stayed on in longhouse 4 after his wife's death because his oldest
daughter, Yámasi (296), is married to her mother's
brother (290) who also has another wife (297). Yámasi
may, therefore, cook and care for her own younger
brothers (315,316,318) and sisters (317,319), as well
as her own child (305).

6. An orphaned child lives with the father's
brother or the mother's sister. There are three
orphaned children (329,330,154) in Figure 5; but, in
this case, the relationship to the others in the
household is not certain.

A new mother lives in a small house away from the
main longhouses. She has a young boy, who may be
related to her in any of various ways, as her companion. In shelter 7 (Figure 6), two classificatory
sisters with infants have their brother's son to help
them. In shelter 9 (Figure 8), a woman and her infant
daughter are accompanied by the husband's nine-year-
old half-brother.

The interior of a traditional longhouse is divided by posts and beams from which to hang hammocks,
but has no interior partitions (Figures 3-5). A central corridor is left open from the door at one end to
the opposite end which is often reserved for the head
of the household and his immediate family of wives and
children. One or more sections of the house nearer the
door are reserved for cooking. Hammocks are hung very
close together with fires on the ground between every
second one or so, which are kindled at night to provide warmth. The different type of construction of a
single large government-built dormitory (Figure 2) has

resulted in a different interior arrangement without
the traditional central corridor.

The general pattern of arranging hammocks is for
the husband to sleep beside his wife with the youngest
child next to or in the same hammock with the mother.
Then usually the hammocks range from the youngest to
the oldest (including orphans) away from the mother.
If there is an older daughter, the next to the youngest may be next to her. Sometimes, with a large family
unit, the husband may sleep in the next house section
along with one of the children. In house 1 (Figure 2),
the husband, Díkibôba (7), has three wives
(24,56,225). The two preferred ones (24,56) are next
to him with the children on either side of them, and
the third wife (225) on the other side of the children. A widowed father (10) sleeps with the youngest
children (39,40) on either side of him.

Named patrilineal groups

Every Suruí is a member of one of three named
groups--the Ngameb, the Ngamngir, or the Makor. The
first two names refer to types of wasp, while the
third refers to a type of bamboo from which arrow
heads are made. Children are members of their father's
group.

Very little is known of the function of these
groups within the society, except that members of each
are perceived as having certain characteristics typical of the group. The Makor, for example, are said to
have bad tempers. All the Suruí have the same style
haircut in front, but each patrilineal group is said
to have had a different hair length in back in the
past. Marriage is practiced within patrilineal groups
as well as between them.

Kinship terms of reference

The Suruí system for classifying kinsmen is, in
its basic form, a symmetrical Dravidian (Lounsbury
1964:1079) system which has been modified by two skewing rules particularly compatible with the preferred
marriage rule of the mother's brother to the sister's
daughter. The system has the following general characteristics:

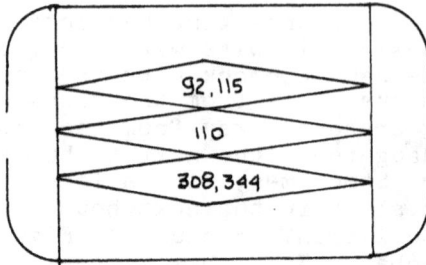

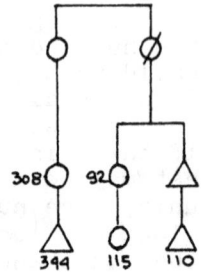

Figure 6. Shelter seven.

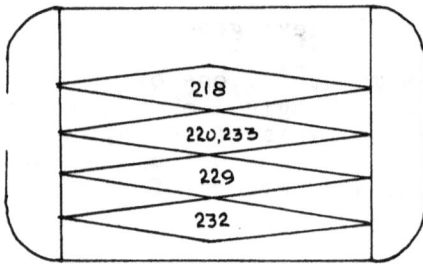

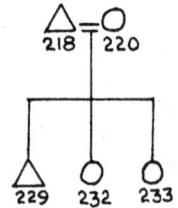

Figure 7. Shelter eight.

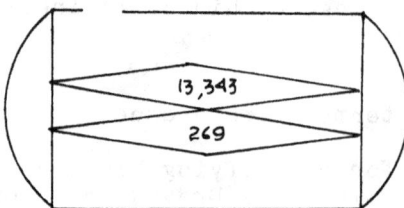

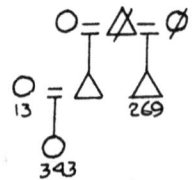

Figure 8. Shelter nine.

1. All kinsmen beyond the first ascending and descending generations are merged under three terms-- two distinguishing the sex of senior kinsmen and one for junior kinsmen.

2. Apart from the skewing to be discussed below, kinsmen of the first ascending generation are distinguished by terms of the bifurcate merging variety, with those of the first descending generation being their regular reciprocals.

3. In ego's generation, parallel cousins are merged with siblings and are distinguished from cross cousins, though a term does also exist to specify parallel cousins as opposed to true siblings.
4. There is no separate set of terms to distinguish affinal from consanguineal kinsmen.

With this brief introduction to the terminological system, we will now return to the beginning for a more detailed discussion.

Grandfather. There is a single term which classes together both lineal male kinsmen of the second ascending generation. This term extends, by Rule 1 (Merrifield 1983), to all males more than one generation distant from ego, as in (2).[4]

(2) ãmõ   PPm(1)   grandfather

Grandmother. A second term denotes grandmothers in a corresponding fashion, merging the two lineal grandmothers with all female kinsmen more than one generation distant from ego, as in (3).

(3) móyá   PPf(1)   grandmother

A skewing rule, however, accounts for the designation of additional kintypes in the grandmother class. The primary kintype in question is the father's sister, who is designated by the grandmother term. As mentioned above, this is particularly appropriate to the preferred marriage rule of the mother's brother to the sister's daughter. The marriage of ego's father to his sister's daughter results in father's sister also being ego's maternal grandmother, as can be seen in (4).

(4)

```
      ┌──────┐
      │      │
  f   │      │
  │   │      │
  f = m
      │
     ego
```

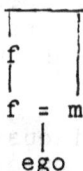

The application of this skewing rule does not depend upon any particular avuncular marriage. There is no other specific term for designating a father´s sister, but rather all real and classificatory sisters of father are termed grandmothers, regardless of actual marriage ties. This first skewing rule may be formally characterized as in (5).

(5) Rule Q: ∅ --> C / PmPf(=G)

Rule Q states that the father´s mother, represented by the string PmPf, is equivalent to the father´s sister, represented as PmPCf, by the addition of C to PmPf. It also states that any expansion of PmPf by application of Rule G is also a proper context for application of Rule Q as long as application of Rule G is limited by the Suruí concept ´parallel´ (designated in 5 by an equals sign [=]). The Suruí definition of parallel extension (Merrifield 1983), which operates here and elsewhere in the system, may be stated as in (6).

(6)   PARALLEL EXTENSION: Within the genealogical chain that links ego to a designated kinsman (alter), wherever there are two kinsmen of the same generation within the chain, those two kinsmen are of the same sex.

In the case of the father´s sister, parallel extension limits further membership in the grandmother class to PmPmPCmCf and PmPfPCfCf for women of one degree of collateral distance, specifically excluding PmPmPCfCf and PmPfPCmCf. Presented graphically, the first two diagrams of (7) represent women of the grandmother class whereas the second two do not. (Asterisk [*] indicates a position in a genealogical chain for which sex of kinsman is not diagnostic of a term.)

(7)
```
    *       *       *       *
    |\      |\      |\      |\
   m m     f f     m f     f m
   | |     | |     | |     | |
   m f     m f     m f     m f
   |       |       |       |
   *       *       *       *
```

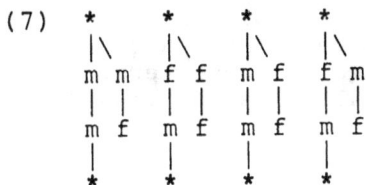

Grandchild. A single term for grandchild is the reciprocal of the two grandparent terms. In its primary sense, it denotes a lineal descendant of ego of the second descending generation. In its first-extended sense (Rule 1), it also denotes a kinsman of a descending generation beyond the first, without reference to lineality, as in (8).

(8) lérad   CC(1)   grandchild

In addition to this first-extended sense of the grandchild term, the reciprocal form of Rule Q, presented in (9), also applies.

(9) Ø --> P / fCmC(=G)

This form of Rule Q states that a woman's fraternal nephew or niece (fPCmC) is equivalent to her agnatic grandchild (fCmC) and that, by one application of Rule =G, the junior kinsman in the first two dyads of (7) are also included within the grandchild class.

Parent and child. Two parent terms distinguish father and mother, while four child terms introduce sex of ego or of kinsman in a variety of ways, as indicated in (10). The man's term for son is homophonous with omâném 'my vagina', spoken by a woman.

(10) lob   Pm(=G)   father
     ni   Pf(=G)   mother
     mug   C(=G)   child
     ném   mCm(=G)   man's son
     âmoy   fCm(=G)   woman's son
     wâid   Cf(=G)   daughter

Parent and child terms all extend beyond their primary ranges to more distant kinsmen of the first ascending and first descending generations, respectively. Two degrees of collateral distance have been verified, but it is assumed that more distantly-removed kinsmen, if identifiable, would be similarly

classified. Extension is limited to parallel kinsmen
by the definition presented above. The parent-child
dyads which fall within the range of these terms, for
up to two degrees of collateral distance are those
presented in (11).

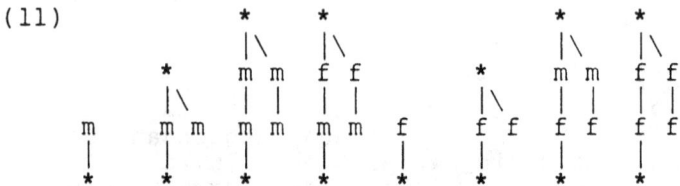

(11)
```
                   *        *                    *       *
                   |\       |\                   |\      |\
        *       m m     f f        *       m m     f f
        |\      | |     | |        |\      | |     | |
  m     m m     m m     m m     f     f f     f f     f f
  |     | |     | |     | |     |     | |     | |     | |
  *     * *     * *     * *     *     * *     * *     * *
```

Uncle, nephew, and niece. There are terms used
between an uncle and his nephew or niece, as indicated
in (12).

(12) nisóa   PfPCm(=G)   uncle
     mahdápid   mPCfC(=G)   man's nephew or niece

The primary sense of the uncle term is the
mother's real brother. The term he uses reciprocally
for his sister's children is based on the term mahd
`man's sister` and ápid `child`. This latter term is a
word usually used by a woman for her own children but
occasionally used by a man for his sister's children
instead of the longer form given in (12).

This dyad is a cross-kinsman dyad since the
genealogical chain between ego and alter fails to meet
the definition of `parallel kinsman` as defined above
for Suruí, viz. mother and mother's brother are two
kinsmen of the same generation within the chain but
are of the opposite sex. On the other hand, extended
senses of these two terms are limited to kinsmen of
greater collateral distance related through parallel
extension only. Kinsmen of the first ascending and
first descending generations related through non-
parallel extension fall outside these kin classes and
are classified with cousins, as will be seen when the
cousin term is introduced.

Sibling. There are six sibling terms, as indicated in (13)--a fully generic term which does not
distinguish distance, seniority, or sex; two terms
which distinguish seniority; two terms used between
opposite-sex siblings; and one term used between same-
sex distant siblings (i.e. parallel cousins).

(13) mór   PC(=G)   sibling
     ngóranãm   ePC(=G)   elder sibling
     ngármēy   yPC=G)   younger sibling
     lóa   fPCm(=G)   woman´s brother
     mahd   mPCf(=G)   man´s sister
     láno   =aPPCCa(=G)   same-sex distant sibling

   Disregarding distinctions of seniority and sex
marked by specific sibling terms, the sibling dyads
for three degrees of collateral distance are represented in (14).

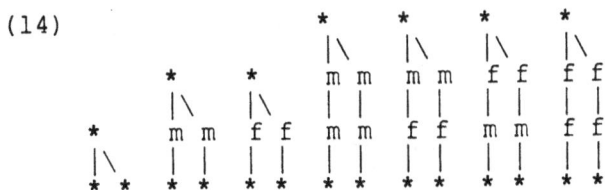

(14)
```
                          *     *     *     *
                          |\    |\    |\    |\
          *     *        m m   m m   f f   f f
          |\    |\       | |   | |   | |   | |
    *    m m   f f      m m   f f   m m   f f
    |\   | |   | |      | |   | |   | |   | |
    * *  * *   * *      * *   * *   * *   * *
```

   Cousin. All cross cousins are classified together
by a single term whose primary sense denotes a kinsman
related to ego through ego´s own parent and an opposite-sex `real` sibling of that parent, as presented
in (15). Another less-common term for the same kinsmen
is otíámakab.

(15) máyxán   xPPCC(2)   cousin

   This term extends (by Rule 2) to kinsmen of the
parent generation, of ego´s generation, and of the
child generation. The Suruí form of Rule 2 is slightly
different from the Rule 2 of Merrifield (1983).   It
operates here only on kintypes of ego´s generation and
applies reciprocally, extending the range of the cousin term to both parent and child generations. A formal
statement of Rule 2 for Suruí is presented in (16).
Suruí cousin dyads up to three degrees of collateral
distance are represented in (17).

(16) RULE 2 (SURUI): Apply part A or B of the filial
     extension rule, or both, without limit except
     that B may only apply (1) the same number of
     times as A, (2) one more time than A, or (3) one
     less time than A.

```
(17)        *     *     *     *     *     *     *     *
           |\    |\    |\    |\    |\    |\    |\    |\
    *       m m   f f   m f   m f   m f   f m   m f   f m
   |\      | |   | |   | |   | |   | |   | |   | |   | |
   m f     m f   m f   m m   f f   m f   m f   *  *   *  *
   | |     | |   | |   | |   | |   | |   | |   |     |
   * *     * *   * *   * *   * *   * *   * *   *     *
```

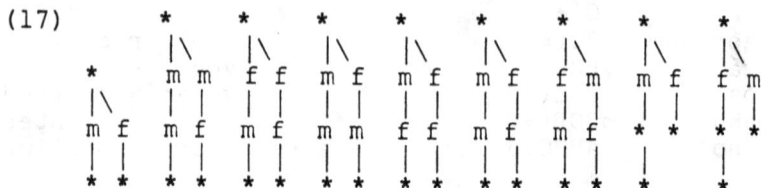

Spouse. A man refers to his wife as omâled ˙my woman˙, and a woman says omaóy ˙my man˙. Alternatively, husband and wife are frequently heard to refer to their spouses as oyígayed. Other terms used by the husband are ólay, onéyzáyed, ólámikoyed (meanings unknown), oméramakab ˙my companion˙, omâlodekär ˙one who looks for my food˙.

A wife may also refer to her husband as omápidlob ˙my child˙s father˙, omaðy (meaning unknown), or the appropriate term for uncle or cousin.

Affinal kinsmen. Most affinal kinsmen are also consanguineal kinsmen and require no special affinal form of reference. There are, however, two special affinal terms in addition to those used for spouses, as indicated in (18).

(18) om   SPC(V,=G)   sibling-in-law
     mári   SPC(V,=G)   sibling-in-law

These terms are used reciprocally (Rule V) between a man or woman and the spouse of his or her sibling. The first term may also refer to son-in-law for either men or women and to father-in-law for men. The extension of these terms needs further investigation.

Residue. There are a few terms which have not yet been identified completely. Ongósó and omórnãra seem to be terms for certain parallel cousins. Onâatin refers to the child of a parallel cousin, based on atin ˙stingy with˙ in the sense of loving something so much that one does not wish to give it up.

Suruí kinship semantics

Apart from secondary extensions, the logical structure of Suruí reference terminology may be defined in terms of five primary conceptual dimensions of meaning: genealogical distance, bifurcation, seniority, relative sex of ego and alter, and sex of kinsman. The Suruí values for each of these dimensions are as in (19).

(19) 1. **Genealogical distance,** with the values:
    1.1 Alter is of ego´s generation.
    1.2 Alter is one generation removed from ego.
    1.3 Alter is more than one generation removed from ego.

2. **Bifurcation,** with the values:
    2.1 Alter is a parallel kinsman--within the genealogical chain that links ego to a designated kinsman, wherever there are two kinsmen of the same generation within the chain, those two kinsmen are of the same sex.5
    2.2 Alter is a cross kinsman--within the genealogical chain that links ego to a designated kinsman, there is at least one pair of opposite-sex kinsmen of the same generation.

3. **Seniority,** with the values:
    3.1 Alter is senior to ego--older than ego if of his generation; otherwise, of an ascending generation.
    3.2 Alter is junior to ego--younger than ego if of his generation; otherwise, of a descending generation.

4. **Relative sex,** with the values:
    4.1 Alter is of the same sex as ego.
    4.2 Alter is of the opposite sex as ego.

5. **Sex of kinsman,** with the values:
    5.1 Alter is male.
    5.2 Alter is female.

By presenting the semantic value of these dimensions for each term in the form of a five-place numeral, the semantic values of the eighteen terms of reference introduced above may be presented as in (20). The structural ranking of the five conceptual dimensions is presented diagrammatically below following a model from systemic linguistics (Berry 1975) and a specific insight of Gary Simons (1983). Relationships between the first three dimensions of meaning are presented in (21).

(20)
ámỗ	PPm(1)	30101	grandfather
móyá	PPf(1)	30102	grandmother
lérad	CC(1)	30200	grandchild
lob	Pm(=G)	21101	father
ni	Pf(=G)	21102	mother
mɨg	C(=G)	21200	child
ném	mCm(=G)	21211	man's son
ámoy	fCm(=G)	21221	woman's son
wáid	Cf(=G)	21202	daughter
nisóa	PfPCm(=G)	22100	uncle
mahdãpid	mPCfC(=G)	22200	man's nephew or niece
mór	PC(=G)	11000	sibling
ngóranãm	ePC(=G)	11100	elder sibling
ngármẽy	yPC(=G)	11200	younger sibling
lóa	fPCm(=G)	11021	woman's brother
mahd	mPCf(=G)	11022	man's sister
láno	=aPPCCa(=G)	11010	same-sex dis. sibling
máyxán	xPPCC(2)	12000	cousin

(21)   1   2   3

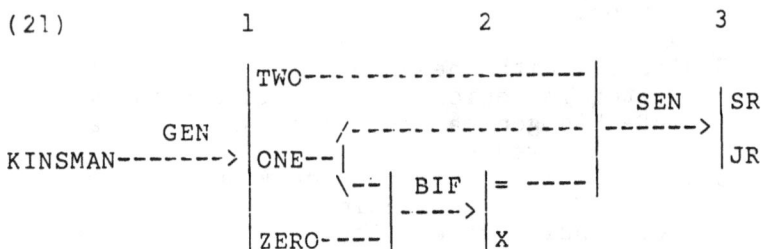

Diagram (21) indicates that Suruí kinsmen are of three types based on genealogical distance (GEN)-- those of more than one generation distance (marked TWO), those of one generation distance (ONE), and those of ego's generation (ZERO). Right-hand arrows (-->) indicate dependency relations between conceptual dimensions (Berry 1975:179ff). In (21), genealogical distance (GEN) is chosen only after choosing KINSMAN. A vertical line, such as the left-most vertical line of (21), indicates a choice between independent, con- trastive values of a semantic dimension. Thus, for example, having chosen GEN, a choice must be made regarding the kinsman's generation (TWO, ONE or ZERO).

The second vertical line in (21), with diagonals at its extremities, represents the simultaneity rela- tion (Berry 1975:181f), to indicate that, having cho- sen ONE, both bifurcation and seniority paths are to

be chosen, both being directly dependent upon the
choice of ONE but neither being dependent, in this
context, on the other. Put another way, all terms for
kinsmen of one generation distance are terminologically distinguished for both bifurcation and seniority.

If TWO is chosen, bifurcation does not figure in
the meaning of terms but seniority does. If ZERO is
chosen, bifurcation figures but seniority does only if
parallel (=) is chosen.

Grandkinsmen. The interrelationships of the three
conceptual dimensions which figure in the classification of grandkinsmen (TWO) aare presented in (22). The
sex of a grandkinsman is seen to be marked only for
senior (SR) grandkinsmen.

(22)

1   2   3   4   5

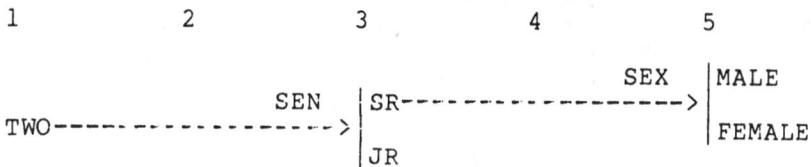

Parent and child. The logical structure for classifying kinsmen one generation distant from ego is
presented diagrammatically in (23). Whereas only three
of the conceptual dimensions come into play for the
definition of grandkinsman terms, all five primary
dimensions are important for kinsmen of the parent and
child generations.

(23)

1   2,3   5   4

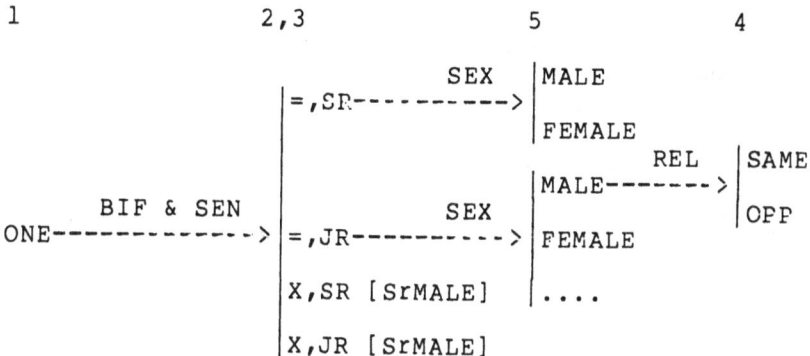

All terms for this set of kinsmen signal both seniority and bifurcate categories. Because of the way sex of kinsman (SEX) and relative sex (REL) depend upon these two dimensions, they are presented in (23) by a displayed network where BIF and SEN are combined and the dimension SEX appears twice. It is possible to consolidate this network to avoid such repetition, but the result is more difficult to read. As (23) shows, parallel senior kinsmen are distinguished by sex. Parallel junior kinsmen, on the other hand, may be distinguished by sex, but there is also a generic term which does not, as indicated in (23) by (....). Parallel junior male kinsmen are further distinguished by relative sex of ego and kinsman.

Cross kinsmen of this set are distinguished only by seniority; but, as it turns out, the senior member of all such cross-kinsman dyads is always male, so that the two terms in question name the `uncle´ and a `man´s nephew or niece´. This limitation to male-senior-member-of-the-dyad is an artifact of Rule Q mentioned previously which defines all corresponding dyads with a female senior kinsman as grandkinsman dyads. There is, thus, a redundancy rule which assigns `senior kinsman of dyad is male´ to these cross-kinsman terms of one generation distance from ego. This rule may be expressed as in (24).

(24) $\emptyset \longrightarrow$ [SrMALE] / ONE & X

The dependency relationship between dimensions four (relative sex) and five (sex of kinsman) is ambivalent in Suruí. In the classification of kinsmen one generation from ego, four is dependent upon five; in the classification of kinsmen of ego´s generation-- as will be seen shortly--five is dependent upon four.

Sibling and cousin. Kinsmen of ego´s (ZERO) generation are illustrated in (25).

(25)

```
1            2          3          4          5

        BIF |X    SEN  |SR
ZERO------> |     -----> |                    |SAME [DISTANT]
            |= -  |JR    REL                  |
            |     --------------------->      |   SEX   |MALE
            |                           |OPP------>     |
            |....                       |               |FEMALE
```

In the first place, parallel kinsmen are distinguished from cousins, the latter constituting a single, undifferentiated set. Secondly, there is a generic term for parallel kinsmen of ego's generation, or
siblings can be more specifically identified by choosing between two other conceptual dimensions--either
seniority or relative sex may be marked in a term, but
not both. If seniority is chosen, there are terms for
senior and junior kinsmen; if relative sex is chosen,
sex of kinsman is also marked for opposite-sex ego.

The term which marks same-sex parallel kinsmen of
ego's generation is limited to distant (nonprimary)
kinsmen of at least two degrees of collateral distance. Collateral distance is here considered a nonprimary conceptual dimension, beyond the five presented above in (19). The assumption is here made that the
near/far distinction ordinarily comes into play
through syntactic modifications rather than as a function of basic terms and that the term for same-sex
distant sibling (láno) represents a lexical exception
rather than the regular structure of the system. The
feature DISTANT is called out whenever the configura-
tion ZERO & = & SAME occurs, as expressed in (26).

(26) $\emptyset$ --> [DISTANT] / ZERO & = & SAME

Extended ranges of reference. Conceptual definitions are excellent for contrasting differences of
meaning between various terms of a system, but they do
not easily characterize differences between primary
and extended ranges of reference of the sort represented by filial extension rules (1, 2, =G) or skewing
rules (Q). The output of such rules is, therefore,
ignored by the conceptual definitions here given. See
Scheffler & Lounsbury (1971) for a componential treatment of a kinship terminology at both primary and
extended ranges.

Kinship terms of address

Suruí terms of address, presented in (27), follow
the same general patterns of extension as terms of
reference, including application of the skewing rule
(Q).

Grandkinsmen. In addition to the use of grandparent terms for true grandparents, they are also used

(vocatively) to call non-Suruí of middle age or older, especially in trying to get such a person's attention.

(27)	amõ	PPm(1)	30101	grandfather
	béya	PPf(1)	30102	grandmother
	mba	Pm(=G,(I,=1))	21001,30201	father, son
	áya	Pf(=G)	21102	mother
	mo, moy	Cm(=G)	21201	son
	wáid	Cf(=1)	21202,30202	daughter
	kokó	PfPCm(=G)	22103	uncle
	ónob	mPCfCm(=G)	22201	man's nephew
	yeéy	mPCfCf(=G)	22202	man's niece
	áre	mPCm(=G)	11011	man's brother
	ínhob	fPCm(=G)	11021	woman's brother
	uhb	PCf(=G)	11002	sister
	ómay	xaPPCCa(2)	12010	same-sex cousin
	némá	xaPPCCb(2)	12020	opposite-sex cousin

The semantic relationships between vocative terms are slightly different from those which exist between reference terms. As can be seen by comparison of (22) and (28), seniority and sex of kinsman become simultaneous in directly addressing grandkinsmen, whereas sex of kinsman was directly dependent upon seniority in reference to grandkinsmen.

(28)

```
  1              2              3             4            5

                           SEN │SR
                          /-----> │
  TWO------------>│       │JR                SEX │MALE
                          \-----------------------------> │
                                                          │FEMALE
```

The fact that grandchildren are not vocatively distinguished from children does not show up in (28), but the reader should note in (27) that grandsons are classified vocatively with fathers and that granddaughters are classified with daughters. This is discussed further in the following section.

Parent and child. The semantic structure of the vocative terms for the parent and child generations differs significantly from that of the corresponding reference terms, and the terms themselves are for the most part different. The basic structure, ignoring certain complexities, is presented in (30).

(30)

```
1                    2,3                4            5

                  | =,SR----------------|
     BIF & SEN    | =,JR----------------|  SEX   |MALE
ONE------------>  |                     | -----> |
                  | X,SR [SrMALE]       |        |FEMALE
                  | X,JR [SrMALE]-------|
```

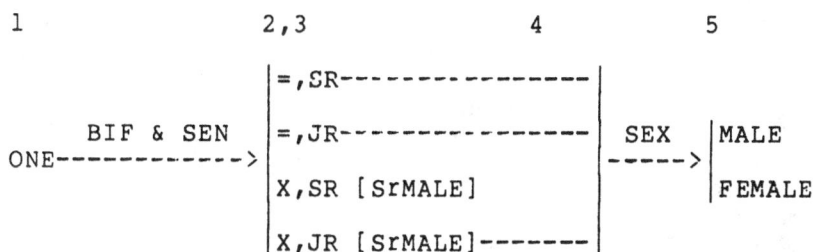

Were it not for Rule Q which reinterprets certain kintypes of one generation distance as grandkinsmen, we would probably have a perfect paradigm of eight terms with all three semantic dimensions--BIF, SEN, and SEX--being simultaneously diagnostic of each in this area of the vocative terminology. With the removal of the indicated kintypes, however, we find redundancy rule (24) applying to add the feature SrMALE to the cross-kinsman kintypes which is incompatible with the feature FEMALE, thereby precluding complete symmetry. The relative sex of ego and kinsman is not a factor in these address terms as it is for the corresponding parallel junior males in reference.

There are additional complexities, however, especially in regard to the extension of the father and daughter terms to include sons, grandsons, and granddaughters. The father term is the more complex of the two. It is self-reciprocal by Rule I (Merrifield 1983:384), which is to say that the reciprocal of Pm is, in this case, Cm. Rule I is associated with filial extension of type =1, which extends Cm to all parallel male kinsmen of descending generations. This extended range parallels that of the daughter term, which ranges over all parallel female kinsmen of descending generations.

The fact that Surui never distinguishes bifurcate categories for kinsmen of more than one generation distance from ego comes into play here. This fact was expressed implicitly in (21) and may be expressed explicitly by a redundancy rule, as in (31). The result is that these two terms contrast with cross kinsman terms at one generation distance from ego but not beyond one generation.

(31) X --> = / TWO

Sibling and cousin. The structure of vocative terms for ego's generation is presented in (32). The semantic structure of sibling and cousin terms in direct address is substantially different from that of reference, as can be seen by comparing (25) and (32). The sibling terms of reference which mark seniority do not have vocative counterparts at all. Furthermore, sex of kinsman dominates relative sex in vocative usage, the reverse of the situation in reference. In the case of sibling terms of address, relative sex of ego is marked for male kinsman only; in the case of cousins, relative sex is marked but sex of kinsman is not.

(32)

```
1               2           3           5           4

        BIF    |X-- -------- -------- ---------- |  REL  |SAME
ZERO------>    |                                 | ----->|
               |                      |MALE      |       |OPP
               |             SEX      |          |
               |=  ---------- ---- -->|
               |                      |FEMALE
```

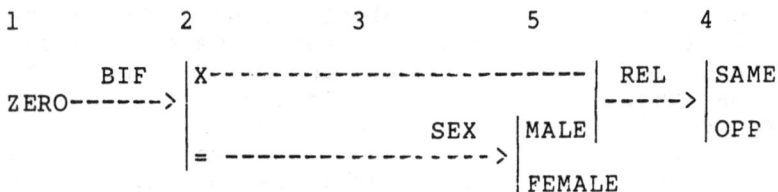

The vocative terms for siblings are only used after puberty. Until puberty, children call each other áre, which is homophonous with a sibling term, but they do so without regard for sex or even kinship. A prepubescent girl may call a male sibling of any age moé, and children of either sex may call a sister ámakűy. A child of either sex may call a pubescent girl akápeáb until she has a child of her own.

NOTES

[1]
    The data for this paper were collected by CB, in collaboration with her husband, Willem Bontkes, from January through March and June through November of 1974 and verified in July of 1984 on the FUNAI Post 'Sete de Setembro' as part of a long-term field

project being carried out under contracts held between
the Summer Institute of Linguistics, the Ministry of
the Interior, the National Indian Foundation (FUNAI),
and the National Museum. Although many individuals
were interviewed, the primary source of data was
Ngasóter, a young man of about 22 years of age. WRM
assisted in the analysis and description. Thanks are
due Willem Bontkes for his participation with CB in
the field research among the Suruí and for drawing the
figures for this presentation.

Suruí phonemes include vowels /i e u [ɨ] a o/,
nasalization /~/, vowel length /h/, obstruents /p t z
[ć] k b d j g/, nasals /m n nh [ñ] ng/, fricatives /s
[ɵ] x [ś]/, liquids /l r/, semivowels /w y/, and
tones: high /'/ and low (unmarked).

This contact has been described by von Puttkamer
(1971), at which time the Suruí were still being
referred to as Cinta Larga. At the time of contact,
there were an estimated 600-800 Suruí living in a
small number of villages two days' walk from the Post.
During the first few years after contact, the Suruí
kept visiting the Post at regular intervals. Then when
contagious diseases struck, they realized their need
of permanent medical help and gradually moved to the
Post where they lived and made their fields until
1983. Since that time they have taken over the coffee
plantations left by Brazilian settlers who were put
off indigenous land in 1981. Except for three families
who were still at the Post in July, 1984, the Suruí
are now spread out over a 20-kilometer area in small
family groups or, in some cases, larger extended families. Their main sources of income are the sale of
coffee and the rubber they tap in the jungle within
the demarcated indigenous area.

A census taken in July, 1984, of the group scat-
tered around the Post Sete de Setembro counts 235
Suruí plus 14 women and children from other indigenous
groups who are married to Suruí men or who are related
to those who are married to Suruí men. The group which
lived at Espigão d'Oeste in 1974 moved to a post
called Linha 14 in 1978. Their population has probably
increased, but there is no recent census.
    3
    A recent discussion of sister's daughter mar-
riage in a Carib-speaking community of lowland South

America, with accompanying bibliography on the subject, may be found in Thomas (1979).
    4
    Terms of reference occur with a preposed pro-
noun. The first person singular pronoun takes the form
o- with all terms except those for grandmother, grandfather, man's son, woman's son, and daughter, in which
case it is oma-. The terms for grandmother and man's
son begin with consonants and do not alternate mor-
phophonemically with a change of pronoun. Grandfather
and woman's son begin with `a´ which blends with oma-.
The term wáid `daughter´ drops the w and follows this
same pattern. Without attempting a full description
here, the following alternations occur: m --> p, n -->
t or z, ng --> k, l --> x or s, n --> nh, and y --> x.
    5
    Though either ego or his designated kinsman may
be one of the generation peers whose sex is relevant
within a given genealogical chain, these definitions
are deliberately meant to exclude reference to sex of
ego and his designated kinsman when they are themselves generation peers. In such a case, treat them as
not `within the chain´ for purposes of the definition.

REFERENCES

Berry, Margaret. 1975. An introduction to systemic
    linguistics 1: structures and systems. New York:
    St. Martin's Press.

Lounsbury, Floyd G. 1964. The structural analysis of
    kinship analysis. In H. G. Lunt (ed.), Proceed-
    ings of the Ninth International Congress of Lin-
    guists, 1073-93. The Hague: Mouton and Co.

Merrifield, William R. 1983. On the formal analysis of
    kinship terminologies. In F. Agard et al. (eds.),
    Essays in honor of Charles F. Hockett. Cornell
    contributions to linguistics 5:371-405.

Scheffler, Harold W. and Floyd G. Lounsbury. 1971. A
    study in structural semantics: the Sirionó kin-
    ship system. Englewood Cliffs: Prentice-Hall,
    Inc.

Simons, Gary. 1983. Semantic reconstruction and change
    in the kinship systems of the Southeast Solomons.
    Paper presented at the 15th Pacific Science
    Congress, Dunedin, New Zealand.

Thomas, David John. 1979. Sister's daughter marriage among the Pemon. Ethnology 18.61-70.

von Puttkamer. 1971. Brazil protects her Cinta Larga Indians. National Geographic 140:420-44.

COGUI KINSHIP

Linda Gawthorne
Summer Institute of Linguistics, Colombia

The Cogui people (also known as Kogi, Kagaba and Cagaba) live on isolated farms on the northern and western slopes of the Sierra Nevada de Santa Marta in northern Colombia, South America. Their population is generally estimated at 3,000-5,000 although some estimates are as high as 10,000. Their language, Cogui, is a member of the Chibchan language family, with the closest relationship being to Arhuaco and Malayo (see Matteson, et al 1972). These languages are also spoken in the Sierra Nevada de Santa Marta, and the groups share many cultural similarities. Most Coguis are monolingual. They maintain their own distinctive customs and clothing and are not acculturated to the national culture of Colombia to any significant degree. For a more detailed description of Cogui culture see Reichel-Dolmatoff (1950-51).1

Cogui world view divides the universe into different kinds of people. The basic distinction is between Coguis (they refer to themselves as kággaba `people´) and non-Coguis. Within the group of Coguis are those that are kinsmen (gahã `family´) and those that are nonkinsmen (axautshi `different´). This is an important distinction, since Coguis may only marry nonkinsmen. Outside of the circle of those who are Coguis are other indigenous groups (axautshi kággaba `different people´) and nonindigenous peoples of Colombia (zhaldi `Colombian´). The Cogui word saná can be translated as `race´. Coguis are quite careful in identifying a person´s `race´, and Coguis do demonstrate a measure of prejudice against those who are not Cogui. The Coguis have more contact with the Arhuaco (pebu) and Malayo (wiwa) peoples than with any other indigenous peoples of Colombia and so have Cogui words with which to refer to them. Guajiro and Chimila peoples, other groups the Coguis are aware of because they live close to the Sierra Nevada, are referred to by Spanish loan words.

One use of the sibling terms does have to do with Cogui world view. They believe they were created before all other races of people, and refer to themselves as duwékue 'older brothers' and to all others--indigenous and nonindigenous peoples alike--as nanikue 'younger siblings'.

Much of Cogui conversation revolves around the family, and kinship terms were some of the first Cogui words that the author learned. Coguis use names very rarely and denote one another both referentially and vocatively by kinship terms.

Terms used in reference to kinsmen are discussed in the first two sections of the paper. These terms always occur with one of the possessive pronouns na- 'my', mi- 'your', or a 'his, her'; but since the presence of these pronouns is associated with a variety of morphophonemic changes to the terms, I present the latter without pronouns. Terms used in direct address to kinsmen do not always occur with pronouns. They are discussed in the third section of the paper.

Filial kinsmen

Grandkinsmen. Three grandkinsman terms distinguish the sex of 'grandparent' but disregard the sex of 'grandchild', as indicated in (1). They extend lineally to ascending and descending generations (by Rule L). The word for grandfather is used in a broader sense to mean ancestors and the word grandchild is used to mean descendents. The term for 'grandfather' is also the term for 'Cogui priest' and the term for 'grandmother' is the term for 'wife of Cogui priest'. The vocative terms for 'priest' and 'grandfather', however, are different.

(1)	mama	PPm(L)	grandfather
	saxa	PPf(L)	grandmother
	tukua	CC(L)	grandchild

Parent and child. Four parent and child terms, listed in (2), do not extend beyond primary kintypes. Two terms distinguish the sex of 'parents', and two terms the sex of 'children'. Either the term for 'father' or the term for 'mother' can be pluralized to refer to both parents. To refer to all of one's children, however, only the plural of the term for 'son' may be used. The unpossessed word for 'daughter' means 'woman'; the unpossessed word for 'mother' can also mean 'source'.

(2)	jate	Pm	father
	jaba	Pf	mother
	sukkua	Cm	son
	munzhi	Cf	daughter

Siblings. Four terms, listed in (3), are used to classify all collateral kinsmen. Relative age, not generation, is the criterion used in classifying such kinsmen. One term is used for any older brother, uncle, nephew or male cousin and can roughly be translated 'older male collateral kinsman'. Another term is used for any older sister, aunt, niece or female cousin. Sex of ego and alter are both significant only in the case of younger siblings of a male ego. Two terms do this in a disjunctive manner. The term for 'younger brother' is also used, by female ego only, to denote a 'younger sister', whereas a male uses a second term for 'younger sister'. This disjunction is handled in (3) by designating the primary range of the 'younger brother' term as yPCm, and expressing the disjunction as a rule of equivalency as in Rule Q below.

Rule Q: f --> m / yfPC__

which may be read: "For female ego, a younger sister is equivalent to a younger brother."

(3)	duwé	ePCm(0)	elder brother
	nu	ePCf(0)	elder sister
	nani	yPCm(0,Q)	younger brother
	jasʉ	ymPCf(0)	man's younger sister

We have not to date found a phrase by which Coguis distinguish true siblings and cousins, if indeed they do so. In gathering genealogical data, we usually resort to asking if two people have the same mother or father.

Adjectives · (dueba 'older male' or wezhu 'older female') can be added to elder sibling terms, resulting in duwé dueba 'old elder brother' and nu wezhu 'old elder sister', to refer to a kinsman approxi-

mately twenty or more years older than ego. Coguis do
not keep track of their ages in any way except in
knowing who is older or younger than they are. The
Coguis at this point are still nearly an entirely
illiterate society, but have shown much interest in
having us keep records of birth dates on their children. Parents have hiked as much as six hours to our
house so that we can record a birth.

Another adjective, nauwa `a little bit´, can
optionally be added to sibling terms resulting in
`sort of or a little bit my brother nauwa nattuwė,
etc. to denote those kinsmen that are further removed
from ego such as second or third cousins. This same
adjective can also qualify the in-law terms for the
corresponding siblings.

Affinal kinsmen

Parents-in-law and children-in-law. Five terms
for parents-in-law and children-in-law listed in (4)
distinguish the sex and genealogical distance of
parents-in-law, but not that of child-in-law which
also extends to grandchild-in-law. The required modi-
fiers that distinguish grandparents-in-law from
parents-in-law are the same as those used for older
collateral kinsmen, and can be used with parents
terms, as an alternate means of referring to grandparents. The parent-in-law/child-in-law relationship
is an important one to Coguis, especially that of a
man to his wife´s parents. A son-in-law is required to
do bride service upon marriage, and even after this
service is ended he has a large share of responsibility in taking care of his in-laws. Cogui morality
dictates that a good man take care of his in-laws.

(4)	juazgui dueba	SPPm(L)	grandfather-in-law
	gagi wezhu	SPPf(L)	grandmother-in-law
	juazgui	SPm(L)	father-in-law
	gagi	SPf(L)	mother-in-law
	juazi	CS(L)	child-in-law

Siblings-in-law. There are four Cogui terms for
siblings-in-law, and a fifth for co-in-law, as listed
in (5).

```
(5)  noma          mSPCm(V,0)      man's brother-in-law
     augui         fSPCm(V,0)    woman's brother-in-law
     jualbi        mSPCf(V,0)       man's sister-in-law
     zuwí          fSPCf(V,0)     woman's sister-in-law
     maushi        SPCS(0)                     co-in-law
```

The sibling-in-law terms specify sex of ego as well as sex of alter. The co-in-law term is self-reciprocal (Rule V) and makes no sex distinction. When alter is male, adjectives can optionally be added for young (sukkua `child') and old (dueba `old male'). These terms are added with respect to the relative age difference between ego and alter. These terms all extend collaterally in the same way as the sibling terms to the spouse of any kinsman referred to as a `sibling' (Rule 0).

Stepkinsmen. A full range of terms exists in Cogui for stepkinsmen, as listed in (6). These terms are used frequently because Cogui marriages are exceptionally fragile. Second and third marriages are not uncommon. These terms extend lineally (Rule L). No terms seem to exist for stepsiblings, and they are referred to as someone else's children.

```
(6)  jate zhakka      PSm(L)            stepfather
     jaku             PSf(L)            stepmother
     sukkualdakka     SCm(L)               stepson
     munzhi zhakka    SCf(L)         stepdaughter
```

Stepkinsmen-in-law. Three terms for stepkinsmen-in-law, listed in (7), are modified forms of in-law terms. Two of these terms distinguish the sex of stepparents-in-law; the third refers to the stepchild-in-law without reference to sex.

```
(7)  juazgui zhakka    SPSm(L)      stepfather-in-law
     gagi zhakka       SPSf(L)      stepmother-in-law
     juazi zhakka      SCS(L)       stepchild-in-law
```

Spouses. The term for spouse, listed in (8) is self-reciprocal, and is used with a possessive pronoun. The unpossessed form also refers to several kinds of talismans which seem to have some kind of protection function in common. A second option for referring to a spouse is as `my man' nají sigí or `my woman' nají munzhi. The free form of the possessive pronoun is used in these cases, whereas all other kinship terms are possessed by using the bound form of the possessive. The bound form of the possessive pronoun when combined with woman means `my daughter`; the free form when combined with woman means `my wife`.

A Cogui man is allowed to have two wives and several have three, though the community frowns on this. Because of this, there is a term in Cogui for my husband's other wife.

(8) sewá   S   spouse
     nemá   fSSf   co-wife

Past spouses are referred to as nasewa nane `my old or abandoned wife`. Past co-wives may also be referred to using the same adjective.

Vocative terms

Vocative kinship terms are commonly used in Cogui. A vocative kinship term, if applicable, is nearly always used as part of the greeting. Most vocative terms are the same as corresponding referential terms, but four, in particular, as listed in (9) have a wider vocative usage than is true in the referential system.

Jate `father` is used vocatively not only for one's father but also for grandfather and corresponding in-laws. Jaba `mother` is used in the same way. Sukua `son` is used not only for one's son but also for grandsons and interestingly enough, not for corresponding in-laws, but rather for corresponding stepkinsmen; and similarly for the daughter term.

(10) jate   Pm(L,S-)   father
     jaba   Pf(L,S-)   mother
     sukua   Cm(L,S-)   son
     munzhi   Cf(L,S-)   daughter

These same four terms may vocatively be extended to other socially proximal kinsmen or nonkinsmen. The extended vocative use of these terms seems to have to do with a close, caring relationship. Terms for son and daughter are often used in this more extended sense, and older siblings, especially, may be heard to call younger siblings `son` or `daughter`.

Other vocative usage is quite close to the referential system, the basic difference being the use of a possessive pronoun. Pronouns are always used in the referential system; in the vocative system they are used with some terms and not with others. Those terms that do not take a possessive pronoun in vocative usage are jate `father´, jaba `mother´, duwé `elder brother´, and nu `elder sister´. All other terms take a pronoun when used vocatively.

Two terms have different vocative forms. Nu `elder sister´ is heard, but is most commonly said as nuhú. There are two vocative terms for co-wife, one which is the same as the referential term, and one which is completely different, jasaldu.

Nonkinsmen, if they are friends of ego, may be greeted using the vocative terms sa `male friend´ and kukkuí `female friend´. If a person is neither a kinsman nor a friend he is usually not greeted.

Summary

Cogui kinship terminology forms a simple, bilateral system which strictly distinguishes lineal and nonlineal kinsmen. Collateral kinsmen are classified solely on the basis of relative age in relation to ego with sex of alter also being marked as it is in almost all terms, but with a special term for a man's younger sister, the social significance of which can only be speculated upon at this time.

Genealogical generation is overridden altogether for nonlineal kinsmen, and in some cases is not very significant for lineal kinsmen, in the sense that distinctions can optionally be made only by the addition of adjectives which mark age.

A significant number of affinal terms bespeak the importance of in-law and step relatives as well as of the fragility of the Cogui marriage bond.

Kinsmen are all important to a Cogui. Loyalty and responsibility to kinsmen are expected. The importance of family is reflected in the fact that greetings are largely vocative kinship terms. Voluntary ties of affection and social proximity are also important within the kinship system, and in some cases outside of it, as is attested by the extension of vocative terms of primary kinsmen, in the sense of Murdock (1949), to socially proximal persons.

NOTE

1

Data for this paper were gathered informally
while visiting with Cogui friends in the Cogui village, San Antonio de Mamarongo. Data were later
checked on a formal basis with Roberto Nacoguí. The
author has worked among the Coguis since July 1978 as
a member of the Summer Institute of Linguistics along
with her colleagues, Bonnie Brobston and Grace Hensarling. Cogui words are spelled on the basis of Gawthorne and Hensarling (in press) using an orthography
adapted from Spanish, with the following special
cases: nasalization is indicated by tilde (~) over a
nasalized vowel, ʉ is a high back unrounded vowel, ñ
is velar, z is a voiced sibilant, sh is as in English
shoe, zh is the voiced counterpart of sh, x is a
strong fricative similar to spanish j, and h is glottal closure. Stress is penultimate unless marked.

REFERENCES

Gawthorne, Linda and Grace Hensarling. In press.
    Fonología del cogui. Sistemas Fonológicos de
    idiomas colombianos 5.

Matteson, Esther et al. 1972. Comparative Studies in
    Amerindian Languages. The Hague: Mouton.

Murdock, George Peter. 1949. Social Structure. New
    York: The Free Press.

Reichel-Dolmatoff, Gerardo. 1950-51. Los Kogi: Una
    tribu de la Sierra Nevada de Santa Marta, Colom-
    bia. Bogotá: Revista del Instituto Etnológico.

A PRELIMINARY NOTE ON COREGUAJE KINSHIP TERMINOLOGY

Frances Gralow and William R. Merrifield
Summer Institute of Linguistics, Colombia and Dallas

The Coreguaje live along the tributaries of the
Orteguaza River, below Florencia, Caquetá, Colombia,
and along the tributaries of the Caquetá River, below
Puerto Solano, Caquetá. Coreguaje is a Western Tucanoan language spoken by a community of approximately
750-1000 speakers who call themselves Coreguaje, Tama,
or Carijona. The Tamas and Carijonas are descendents
of people who spoke the Tama and Carijona languages,
but who intermarried with the Coreguaje people. For
the purposes of this paper, the entire community will
be referred to as Coreguaje. Related Western Tucanoan
languages include the Siona of Colombia and Ecuador,
Secoya of Ecuador, and Orejón of Peru.1

There are three factors in Coreguaje kinship
which need to be discussed before the terminology can
be presented in detail--bifurcate categories, generational extension, and generational skewing. First, the
bifurcate categories of Coreguaje need to be defined.

Bifurcate categories. Coreguaje is a Dravidian
system with systematic affinities to Suruí of Brazil
(Bontkes and Bontkes 1984), Sirionó of Bolivia (Scheffler and Lounsbury 1971), and Cubeo of Colombia (Morse
1984). These systems have a reduced `parallel` category in comparison to other types of Dravidian terminologies in that, to qualify as a parallel kinsman,
there must be same-sex pairs of linking kinsmen in all
generations above ego and alter. The categories
`parallel` and `cross` may be defined structurally for
Coreguaje as in (1).

PARALLEL (Coreguaje): Within the genealogical
chain that links ego to a designated kinsman,
whenever there are two kinsmen of the same generation within the chain, those two kinsmen are of
the same sex.

43

CROSS (Coreguaje): Within the genealogical chain that links ego to a designated kinsman, tnere is at least one pair of opposite-sex kinsmen of the same generation.

The outworking of tnese definitions, in the way specific terms extend beyond their primary ranges of reference, is described below as each set of terms is introduced; but by way of illustration, the `parallel` (=) kintype dyads for three degrees of collateral distance in ego's generation are presented diagrammatically in (2) and the corresponding cross-kinsman (x) dyads are presented in (3). Since `parallel` may be considered to be the unmarked category of the two, the first-degree collateral dyad--which has no ascending-generation sibling pair--is counted as parallel and is included in (2).

(2)

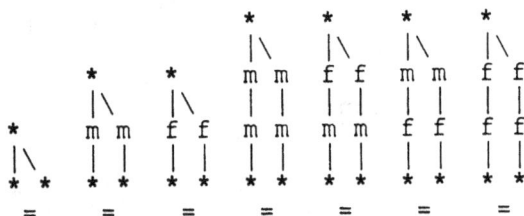

(3)

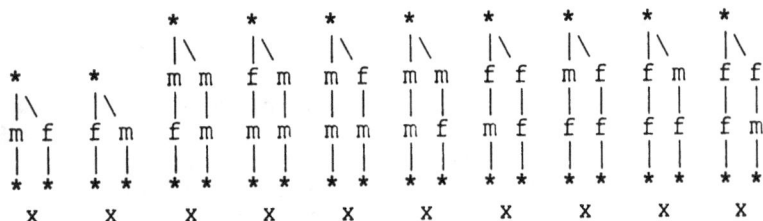

Generational extension. All Coreguaje kinship terms, except those for spouse, extend collaterally beyond primary ranges throughout their corresponding generations. Rule G has been defined (Merrifield 1983) to represent such extension. In terms of PC-string representations of ranges of reference, Rule G generates extended strings by successive additions of PC (one `P` and one `C`) to the center of shorter strings. In the Coreguaje case, Rule G is limited to `parallel` generational extension in the form aPCa which represents the introduction of only same-sex siblings to extend strings. This is so even for the extension of cross-kinsman kintypes. This restricted sense of generational extension is indicated in the following material as Rule =G. Starting at the left of Figures (2) and (3), each further degree of collateral distance represented by dyads to the right represents the application of aPCa--that is, either mPCm or fPCf--to the lesser degree of collateral distance dyads to the left.

Generational skewing. As indicated above, all Coreguaje terms, except spouse terms, extend by Rule =G throughout the generations of their primary ranges. In addition, however, each of these same terms extends to a limited number of kintypes of other generations than that of the primary kintype by a skewing rule of Omaha Type I (Lounsbury 1964). This rule has a citation and reciprocal form. The citation form may be represented formally in terms of PC strings as an expansion rule as in (4).

(4)   Rule Q: Ø --> Cm / PfPC(R)

    Rule Q may be read:

    Mother´s sibling (of either sex) is equivalent to mother´s brother´s child (of either sex)

and represents successive insertions of Cm into strings characterized by having PfPC at their center. It has the effect of transforming PfPC into PfPCmC, PfPCmCmC, PfPCmCmCmC, and so forth, as illustrated in (5).

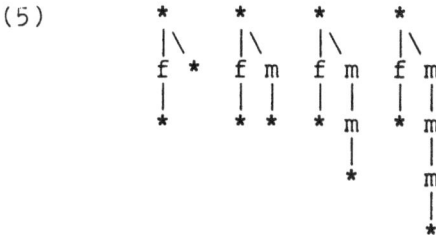

(5)
```
        *       *       *       *
        |\      |\      |\      |\
        f *     f m     f m     f m
        |       | |     | |     | |
        *       * *     * m     * m
                        |       |
                        *       m
                                |
                                *
```

    The reciprocal form (R) of Rule Q is presented in (6).

(6)   Ø --> mP / PCfC

    It may be read:

Sister's child (of either sex) is equivalent to father's sister's child of either sex.

In its reciprocal form, Rule Q represents successive insertions of mP at the center of a string PCfC, transforming it into PmPCfC, PmPmPCfC, PmPmPmPCfC, and so forth, as illustrated in (7), which is a mirror image of (5).

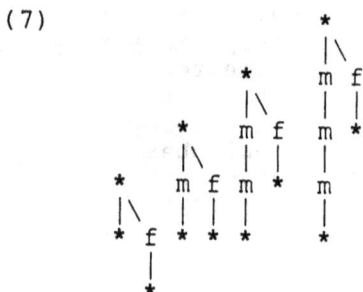

(7)
```
                          *
                         |\
                  *      m f
                 |\      | |
           *     m f     m *
          |\     | |     |
     *    m f m  *       m
    |\    | | |          |
    * f   * * *          *
    |
    *
```

The application of Rule Q, in interaction with Rule =G, has the effect of extending the ranges of terms to many cross-kinsman kintypes otherwise not covered because of the restricted Coreguaje definition of the category 'parallel' and the limitation of Rule G to =G. This will become more clear as individual sets of terms are introduced.2 Since the primary context of application of Rule Q relates to mother's siblings (PfPC), the sets in which terms for these kinsmen participate are presented first in the following sections.

Terms for filial kinsmen

Kinship terms of reference for filial kinsmen fall into five sets: grandkinsmen, parents and children, siblings, and two cross-kinsman sets. We will begin with the cross-kinsman sets.

Cross kinsmen. Two reciprocal sets of three terms each, listed in (8), designate cross kinsmen in Coreguaje. The first set of three names the mother's brother and a man's sister's children, in their primary senses. The second set names the father's sister and a woman's brother's children.

Extension through the first ascending and first descending generations is by parallel extension (=G).

(8)   cha´cha   PfPCm(=G,Q)   uncle

cha´cha	PfPCm(=G,Q)	uncle
u´chaʉ	mPCfCm(=G,Q)	man´s nephew
u´chao	mPCfCf(=G,Q)	man´s niece
pʉ´ko	PmPCf(=G,Q)	aunt
jʉ̃taʉ	fPCmCm(=G,Q)	woman´s nephew
jʉ̃tao	fPCmCf(=G,Q)	woman´s niece

Since, by definition, no lineal kinsman one generation removed from ego can be a cross kinsman, the kintype dyads which correspond to the terms of (8) are those illustrated in (9)--for the first two degrees of collateral distance.

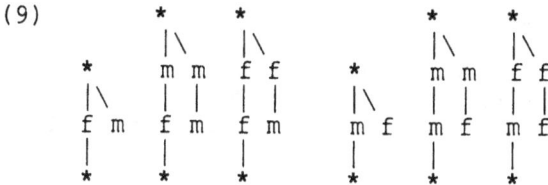

(9)

```
            *     *                *     *
           |\    |\               |\    |\
    *      m m   f f       *      m m   f f
   |\      | |   | |      |\      | |   | |
   f m     f m   f m      m f     m f   m f
   |       |     |        |       |     |
   *       *     *        *       *     *
```

The extension of the mother´s brother term and its reciprocals by Rule Q from primary ranges of reference is illustrated by the dyads of (10). The primary range is presented first, followed by the first three applications of Rule Q, which is perhaps as many applications that would ever be encountered in real life. The mother´s brother term (cha´cha) names the kinsman at the right-hand termini of these strings; the man´s sister´s child terms (u´chaʉ and u´chao) apply to their left-hand termini.

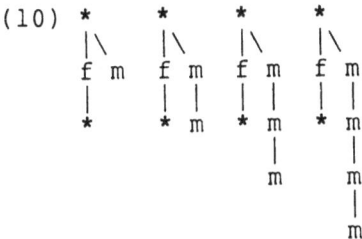

(10)

```
    *       *       *       *
   |\      |\      |\      |\
   f m     f m     f m     f m
   |       | |     | |     | |
   *       * m     * m     * m
                   |       |
                   m       m
                           |
                           m
```

These terms also extend by Rule Q after the application of generational extension (Rule =G). This is illustrated in (11), with the first dyad representing one application of =G in the form fPCf, since the form mPCm does not provide a context to which Q is applicable. The second and third dyads represent the first two applications of the citation form of Q, while the fourth represents one application of Q in its reciprocal form.

The father's sister term and its reciprocals do not extend by Rule Q directly from their primary ranges, but they do so extend from applications of Rule =G in the form fPCf. This is illustrated in (12), in the same fashion as for the mother's brother term and its reciprocals in (11); namely, the first dyad represents one application of =G, the second and third dyads represent two applications of Q in its citation form from the first dyad, and the fourth dyad represents one application of Q in its reciprocal form from the first dyad. The right-hand termini of the dyads represent kinsmen to which the father's sister term (puˊko) applies; the left-hand termini represent kinsmen to which a woman's sister's children (jūtau and jūtao) apply.

(11)   (12)

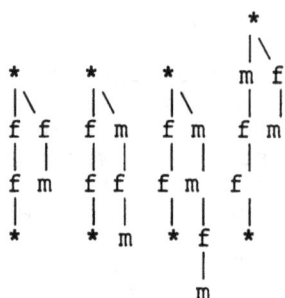   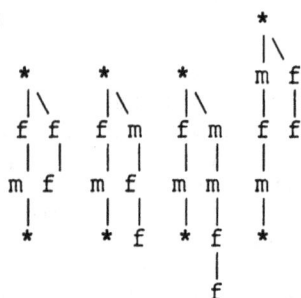

Parent and child terms. Four terms, listed in (13), distinguish seniority and sex of kinsmen of the first generation from ego. These terms are best labelled as parallel, even in their primary denotations, because they contrast directly with the terms for cross kinsmen discussed immediately above.

(13) jaˊku   =Pm(=G,Q)   father
     jaˊko   =Pf(=G,Q)   mother
     chīiu   =Cm(=G,Q)   son
     chīio   =Cf(=G,Q)   daughter

The corresponding kintype dyads for these terms are presented graphically in (14).

Parent and child terms extend by Rule Q in exactly the same way as indicated above for cross-kinsman

(14)

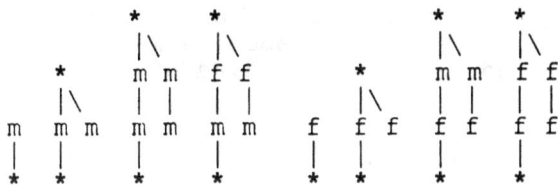

terms, mother paralleling mother's brother and father paralleling father's sister, as can be seen by comparing the following illustrations with (10) through (12) above. The term for mother (ja'ko) extends from its first degree collateral extension (which corresponds to the primary range of the mother's brother term) by Rule Q, as indicated in (15), with the child terms (chĩiʉ and chĩio) as its reciprocals.

(15)

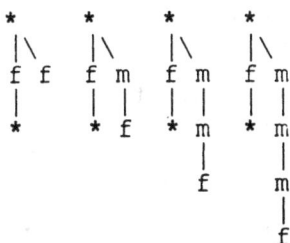

It also extends from further collateral degrees by Rule Q, the second degree being illustrated in (16). The first dyad of (16) represents two applications of Rule =G to the primary denotation of the term (and its reciprocals). The second and third dyads represent two applications of the citation form of Q to the first dyad; the fourth dyad represents one application of the reciprocal form of Q to the first dyad.

(16)

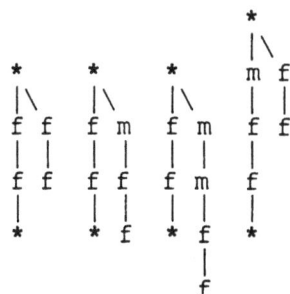

Similarly, the father term, and the same child terms, extend by Q from their second degree collateral kintypes, indicated as the first dyad of (17).

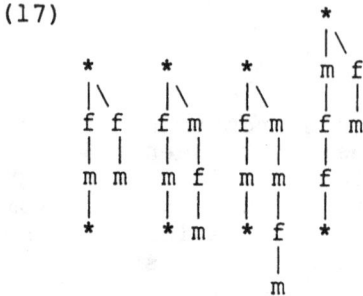

(17)
```
                                    *
                                    |\
        *       *       *           m f
        |\      |\      |\          | |
        f f     f m     f m         f m
        | |     | |     | |         |
        m m     m f     m m         f
        |       | |     | |         |
        *       * m     * f         *
                                    |
                                    m
```

Sibling terms. Four terms, listed in (18), name siblings, distinguishing seniority and sex. In the case of kinsmen of ego´s generation, seniority is calculated on the basis of the order of birth of the true siblings in the genealogical chain that links ego to alter, and not directly in terms of the order of birth of ego and alter themselves except in the case when they are true siblings.

(18) a´chʉ   =ePCm(=G,Q),PPPm(PC,=G)   elder brother
     a´cho   =ePCf(=G,Q),PPPf(PC,=G)   elder sister
     cho´jeʉ   =yPCm(=G,Q),CCCm(PC,=G) younger brother
     cho´jeo   =yPCf(=G,Q),CCCf(PC,=G) younger sister

The terms of (18) also extend, as indicated, to great-grandkinsmen, with the senior terms applying to kinsmen of the third ascending generation and the junior terms to kinsmen of the third descending generation. The kintype dyads over which these terms range, for ego´s generation, are illustrated in (19).

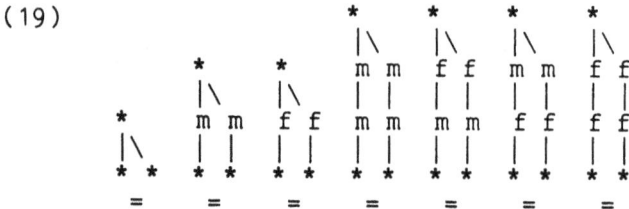

(19)
```
                        *       *       *       *
                        |\      |\      |\      |\
            *       *   m m     f f     m m     f f
            |\      |\  | |     | |     | |     | |
        *   m m     f f m m     m m     f f     f f
        |\  | |     | | | |     | |     | |     | |
        * * * *     * * * *     * *     * *     * *
          =     =     =     =     =     =     =
```

Sibling terms extend by Rule Q in conjunction with one or more applications of =G in its feminine form (fPCf), as illustrated in (20), where the first dyad represents one extension by fPCf, dyads two and three represent two subsequent applications of Q in its citation form, and dyads four and five represent two applications of Q in its reciprocal form.

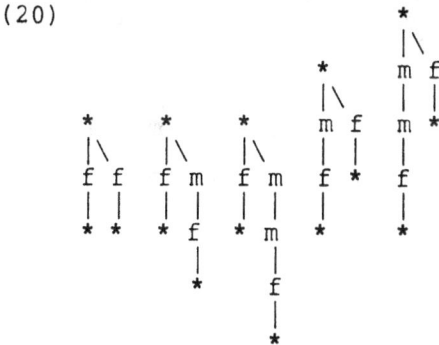

(20)
```
                                    *
                                    |\
                          *         m f
                          |\        | |
         *     *     *     m f       m *
         |\    |\    |\    | |       |
         f f   f m   f m   f *       f
         | |   | |   | |   |         |
         * *   * f   * m   *         *
               |     |
               *     f
                     |
                     *
```

As terms for great-grandkinsmen, sibling terms extend to first degree collaterals without reference to bifurcate categories, as indicated in (21), by a single application of PC. Further collateral extension in the third generation from ego, however, is limited to parallel extension by Rule =G. Rule Q would presumably also apply if kinsmen in appropriate genealogical relationships were known, but we have not been able to verify this by actual cases.

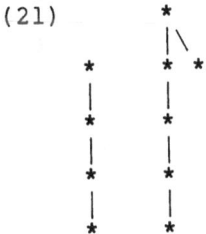

(21)
```
               *
               |\
         *     * *
         |     |
         *     *
         |     |
         *     *
         |     |
         *     *
```

Grandkinsmen terms. Four terms for grandkinsmen, listed in (22), mark seniority and sex of grandkinsmen.

(22) cu˙eʉ   PPm(PC,=G,Q)   grandfather
      cu˙eo   PPf(PC,=G,Q)   grandmother
      najeʉ   CCm(PC,=G,Q)   grandson
      najeo   CCf(PC,=G,Q)   granddaughter

They extend to first degree collateral kinsmen of the second generation from ego by the simple addition of PC, without respect to bifurcate categories, and to more distant collaterals of the second generation from ego by Rule =G. The kintype dyads for lineal grand-kinsmen and two degrees of collateral distance which fall within the range of these terms are illustrated graphically in (23). The small size of the population, and the frequent intermarriage of relatively close kinsmen make it unlikely that a relationship in the second generation would often be traced beyond two degrees of collateral distance although this could be theoretically done without difficulty.

(23) 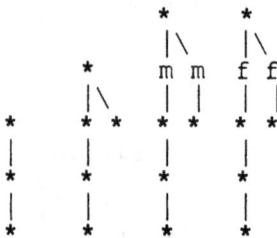 (24)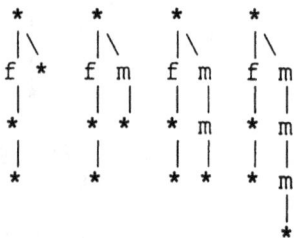

Grandkinsman terms extend from their first degree collateral kintypes by Rule Q when the linking kinsman in the second ascending generation is female, as indicated in (24), where the first dyad represents extension by PC, and the rest represent three successive applications of Q. The grandparent terms name the kinsmen represented by the right-hand termini of these dyads; grandchild terms name the kinsmen represented by the left-hand termini.

As in the case of other terms, grandkinsman terms theoretically also extend from second degree collateral kintypes through females in the manner illustrated in (25), although seldom would kinsmen so distant be known, if ever, given current demographic conditions.

Terms for affinal kinsmen

Although almost all affinals are also related to one another through filial links, nearer affinal relationships take priority through the use of affinal terms, of which there are three reciprocal sets-- parents/children-in-law, siblings-in-law, and spouses.

(25)
```
                               *
                               |\
      *       *       *        m  f
      |\      |\      |\       |  |
      f  f    f  m    f  m     f  *
      |  |    |  |    |  |     |
      *  *    *  f    *  m     *
      |       |  |    |  |     |
      *       *  *    *  f     *
      |       |       |  |     |
      *       *       *  *     *
```

Parent- and child-in-law terms. Two terms, listed in (26), are used reciprocally (Rule R) between a father-in-law and his child-in-law of either sex, on the one hand, or between a mother-in-law and her child-in-law of either sex, on the other. In reference to spouse´s parent, these terms extend by Rules =G and Q in the same fashion as parent terms; and, conversely, to spouse of child in the same fashion as child terms.

(26) vaʉ   =SPm(R,=G,Q)   father/child-in-law
     vao   =SPf(R,=G,Q)   mother/child-in-law

Sibling-in-law terms. Two sibling-in-law terms, listed in (27), distinguish the sex of spouse´s sibling and sibling of spouse, defining ´sibling´ in the same primary and extended senses as for filial kinsmen.

(27) je´oʉ   =SPCm(V,=G,Q)   brother-in-law
     je´oo   =SPCf(V,=G,Q)   sister-in-law

Spouse terms. Finally, two terms, listed in (28), are used between husband and wife. They are unique among Coreguaje kinship terms in not extending beyond their primary denotations.

(28) ʉ̃jʉ   Sm   husband
     rʉ̃jo   Sf   wife

NOTES

1

Data for this paper were gathered in the village of Maticurú, between the years 1975 and 1983 by Frances Gralow as a part of a long-range project of the Summer Institute of Linguistics. Principal language

consultants were María Pizarro de Lozano, Alicia Gar-cía Pizarro, Nicéforo Lozano Ibáñez and Fabián García Moreno. The orthography used in this paper for Core-guaje is based on Young, Cook, and Gralow (n.d.), but adapted to Spanish as follows: c and qu represent /k/, k is /kh/, apostrophe (´) is glottal stop, ʉ is /ɨ/, j is /h/, ch is /j/, and tilde (~) represents nasaliza-tion.
2
Those familiar with Lounsbury´s work will recog-nize that his skewing rules are ordered in respect to other rules of extension. More will be said about this later; but by limiting generational extension to =G for Coreguaje, Rules Q and =G need not be ordered in respect to one another.

REFERENCES

Bontkes, Carolyn & William R. Merrifield. 1985. On Suruí (Tupian) social organization. This volume.

Lounsbury, Floyd G. 1964. A formal analysis of the Crow- and Omaha-type kinship terminologies. In W. H. Goodenough (ed.), Explorations in cultural anthropology, 351-93. New York: McGraw-Hill.

Merrifield, William R. 1983. On the formal analysis of kinship terminologies. In F. Agard, G. Kelley, M. Makkai, and V. B. Makkai, eds., Essays in honor of Charles F. Hockett (=Cornell contributions to linguistics 5), F. Van Coestsem and L. R. Waugh (gen. eds.). Leiden: E. J. Brill. Pp. 371-404.

Morse, Nancy L. 1985. Cubeo kinship. This volume.

Scheffler, Harold W. and Floyd G. Lounsbury. 1971. A study in structural semantics: the Sirionó kin-ship system. Englewood Cliffs: Prentice-Hall, Inc.

Young, Carolyn Muller, Dorothy M. Cook, and Frances L. Gralow. n.d. Fonemas del coreguaje. To appear in: Sistemas fonológicos de idiomas Colombianos 5.

TUCANO (TUCANOAN) KINSHIP TERMINOLOGY

Marie Goehner, Birdie West & William R. Merrifield
Summer Institute of Linguistics, Colombia & Dallas

This paper explores the terminological system of kinship reference of the Tucano people of Acaricuara, Colombia.1 The Tucano people live near the southeastern frontier of Colombia, along the Paca, Papurí, and Vaupés Rivers in the Vaupés District (Comisaría), as well as in nearby Brazil. The Tucano people call themselves Dasea ´toucan´, the apparent explanation for the name by which we know them. Their language, also called Tucano, is a member of the Eastern Tucanoan Family, and serves as a lingua franca for the many distinct language communities of the area.

The Tucano language community consists of a single, exogamous, patrilineal phratry, made up of approximately twenty-six patrilineal sibs. Since the phratry is isomorphic with the linguistic community (apart from bilingualism and the use of the language as a lingua franca), wives and mothers of the Tucano speak languages other than Tucano as their first language. The result is a good deal of bilingualism and even multilingualism in the area. Our Tuyuca language consultant, María Valencia de Cordero, whose mother was Tucano, was every bit as familiar with the Tucano kinship system as her Tucano husband, perhaps even more adept than he in deciding which term we were asking about in our formal inquiry. The reader may wish to consult the literature for further information relating to the linguistic situation in the Vaupés (as for example, Sorenson 1967).

This paper begins with a description of the system of kinship reference, followed by a section on the vocative use of kinship terms. The identification of the differences between the two systems in Tucano has been somewhat difficult for at least two reasons.

55

In the first place, it is not always clear when a term is being used vocatively or in reference, since a pronoun is not invariably used in reference. The Tucano are comfortable in saying such things as, "I saw mother down at the river," which is perfectly clear in a real situation but not always so clear when situations are somewhat contrived when in the process of formal inquiry. Fortunately, Birdie West and her partner Betty Welch have had years of listening to kinship usage in such live situations; but unfortunately, no amount of informal listening by an outsider can unravel the complexity of a system like the Tucano system. Formal inquiry has been necessary, and contrived situations have been utilized in order to muster up all of the kinds of people our language consultants might want to refer to or address by a kinship term.

In the second place, the Tucano people prefer and practice bilateral cross-cousin marriage--not exclusively, but frequently. Most kinsmen are related to one another in multiple ways. It took us some time to discern which relationships took precedence over which others, and even to realize in many instances that a particular relationship which we as analysts were focussing upon was, in fact, not the one to which our language consultants were responding.

For a while, it was difficult to get our data to hold still; but we now believe we have been able to identify the general nature of Tucano kinship reference and the key differences which exist between vocative and referential use of terms. The following discussion will focus upon the referential use of terms, and the forms presented will be the forms used in reference to third persons. Wherever a reference term is also used vocatively, however, a `v´ follows in parentheses. In the case of a vocative term which is different in form from a corresponding reference term, but which ranges over the same kintypes, it is listed in parentheses following the reference term without further comment. Other cases, where vocative terms range over different kintypes from their referential counterparts, are discussed in a special section after all of the terms of reference have been introduced.

The paper closes with comments regarding the names and locations of Tucano sibs.

Reference terms

Grandkinsmen. Four terms, listed in (1), designate grandkinsmen, with lineal grandfathers, grandmothers, grandsons, and granddaughters being the
respective primary kinsmen. Grandkinsmen are a large
class of kinsmen composed of all filial kinsmen two
or more generations' distance from ego, lineal or
collateral, irrespective of sib affiliation or sex of
linking kinsmen (Rule 1). Terms also extend to all
corresponding affinals, whether stepkinsmen or kinsmen-in-law (Rule S).

(1) ñecã   PPm(1,S)   grandfather
     ñecõ   PPf(1,S)   grandmother
     pãrãmi (v)   CCm(1,S)   grandson
     pãrãmeo (v) CCf(1,S)   granddaughter

Parents and children. Four terms, listed in (2),
denote male and female parents, on the one hand, and
male and female children, on the other. None of the
terms has an extended sense in reference, with the
exception of the daughter term, which is discussed
again further below.

(2) pacã (v)   Pm   father
     pacõ (ma'u)   Pf   mother
     macã (v)   Cm   son
     macõ (v)   Cf   daughter

Siblings. Four agnatic sibling terms, listed in
(3), mark seniority and sex of kinsman.

(3) ma'mi   (v)   ePmCm(Gm)   elder brother
     ma'mio   (v)   ePmCf(Gm)   elder sister
     acabiji (nijiã) yPmCm(Gm) younger brother
     acabijo (numio) yPmCf(Gm)   younger sister

As indicated in (3), these terms are extended to
all agnatic kinsmen of ego's generation by successive
applications of Rule Gm which, theoretically, inserts
an indefinite number of strings of the form PmCm into
the center of a primary string. It is unlikely in
practice, however, that any relationship beyond that
of second cousins--the equivalent of two such
insertions--would ever need to be calculated, because
of the continual reestablishment of closer relationships through bilateral cross-cousin marriage and
sister exchange.

Beyond agnatic kinsmen whose filial relationships to ego are known, sibling terms extend to all members of ego's sib and phratry--that is, to all Tucanos--who are 'considered' to be of ego's generation. When one Tucano meets another of his sib whom he has not previously known, the two discuss genealogical matters to determine how their patrilineal forbears may have been related. Some Tucano men are reported to have extensive knowledge of such matters, while others have less, depending in part upon the apprenticeship their fathers and fathers' brothers have given them in this matter. Within the sib, it is usually possible to identify a known agnatic relationship which then guides subsequent behavior and the use of appropriate terminology.

Seniority is calculated on the basis of the order of birth of the true siblings in the genealogical chain that links ego to alter. If ego and alter are true siblings, it is their own order of birth that matters. If their fathers were true siblings, the son of the older father is senior. If their paternal grandfathers were true siblings, the grandson of the older grandfather is senior, and so forth as far as a known agnatic tie exists.

Beyond known ties within a sib, relationships between Tucanos of different sibs are fixed by convention. Our data on this matter are from Dionisio Cordero of the Ne´rã Põ´rã sib, who--whether for the sake of modesty or not we cannot say--does not claim particular expertise concerning Tucano sibs, even though he was able to name twenty-six of them and name their relationship to his. This information is presented in the last section of the paper.

From the point of view of Dionisio's sib, individuals of the other twenty-five sibs are ranked as 'elder brothers', as 'younger brothers', or as 'grandfathers'. Genealogical discussions take place between individuals who meet for the first time in the same way as indicated above for persons of the same sib. In general, three generations of men of an 'elder brother' sib are classified as 'father's brothers', 'elder brothers', and 'brother's sons' by an adult male of Ne´rã Põ´rã sib. Men of a 'younger brother' sib are classified in a similar fashion, using the 'younger brother' term for the middle generation. Three generations of men of a 'grandfather' sib, on the other hand, would tend to be classified as `grandfathers´, `father´s brothers´, and `elder brothers´, respectively.

Bifurcate categories. Before moving on to the presentation of further data, it is necessary to define the bifurcate categories `parallel´ and `cross´ for Tucano, which displays a Dravidian pattern (Lounsbury 1964:1079) of the Mayoruna subtype (Fields and Merrifield 1980:17). This may be done as in (4).

The characteristic which makes the Mayoruna subtype of Bifurcation unique from that of other well-known systems like that of the Kariera (Romney and Epling 1958), for example, is in the choice of kinsmen in a genealogical chain which are counted in respect to the above definitions.

(4) PARALLEL (MAYORUNA): a kinsman related to ego through a genealogical chain which includes an even number $(0,2,4,...,n)$ of male kinsmen and an even number of female kinsmen.

CROSS (MAYORUNA): a kinsman related to ego through a genealogical chain which includes an odd number $(1,3,5,...,n)$ of male kinsmen and an odd number of female kinsmen.

Tucano only marks bifurcate categories for kinsmen of ego´s generation, the parent generation, and the child generation. In the case of ego´s generation, Mayoruna and Tucano is no different from other systems like Kariera, namely, ego and alter are never included within the count, nor is the common ancestor of ego and alter; all other kinsmen in the chain are counted. In the case of the parent and child generations, however,--and this is where Mayoruna and Tucano differ from Kariera--ego is never counted and alter always is, whether alter is a generation peer of parent or of child. This results in normal sets of parallel and cross kintypes for kinsmen of the parent generation--a sample are listed in (5)--but unexpected ones for kinsmen of the child generation, as indicated in (6).

We can now proceed with the discussion of parallel and cross cousins in Tucano.

Mother´s children. Parallel kinsmen of ego´s generation who are not also agnatic kinsmen and,

(5)
```
         *     *     *     *            *     *     *     *
         |\    |\    |\    |\           |\    |\    |\    |\
   *     m m   f f   f m   m f    *     m m   f f   f m   m f
   |\    | |   | |   | |   | |    |\    | |   | |   | |   | |
   m m   m m   m m   f m   f m   f f   f f   f f   m f   m f
   |     |     |     |     |     |     |     |     |     |
   *     *     *     *     *     *     *     *     *     *
   =     =     =     =     =     =     =     =     =     =

         *     *     *     *            *     *     *     *
         |\    |\    |\    |\           |\    |\    |\    |\
   *     m m   f f   f m   m f    *     m m   f f   f m   m f
   |\    | |   | |   | |   | |    |\    | |   | |   | |   | |
   f m   f m   f m   m m   m m   m f   m f   m f   f f   f f
   |     |     |     |     |     |     |     |     |     |
   *     *     *     *     *     *     *     *     *     *
   x     x     x     x     x     x     x     x     x     x
```

(6)
```
         *     *     *     *            *     *     *     *
         |\    |\    |\    |\           |\    |\    |\    |\
   *     m m   f f   f m   m f    *     m m   f f   f m   m f
   |\    | |   | |   | |   | |    |\    | |   | |   | |   | |
   * m   * m   * m   * f   * f   * f   * f   * f   * m   * m
   |     |     |     |     |     |     |     |     |     |
   m     m     m     m     m     f     f     f     f     f
   =     =     =     =     =     =     =     =     =     =

         *     *     *     *            *     *     *     *
         |\    |\    |\    |\           |\    |\    |\    |\
   *     m m   f f   f m   m f    *     m m   f f   f m   m f
   |\    | |   | |   | |   | |    |\    | |   | |   | |   | |
   * f   * f   * f   * m   * m   * m   * m   * m   * f   * f
   |     |     |     |     |     |     |     |     |     |
   m     m     m     m     m     f     f     f     f     f
   x     x     x     x     x     x     x     x     x     x
```

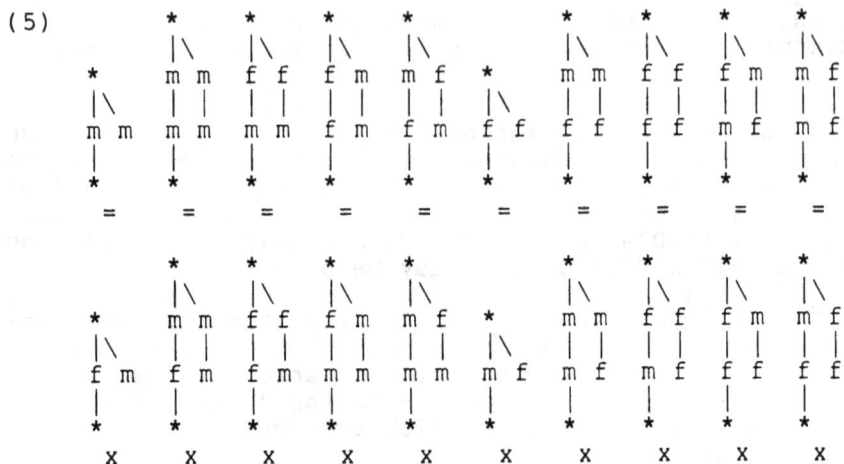

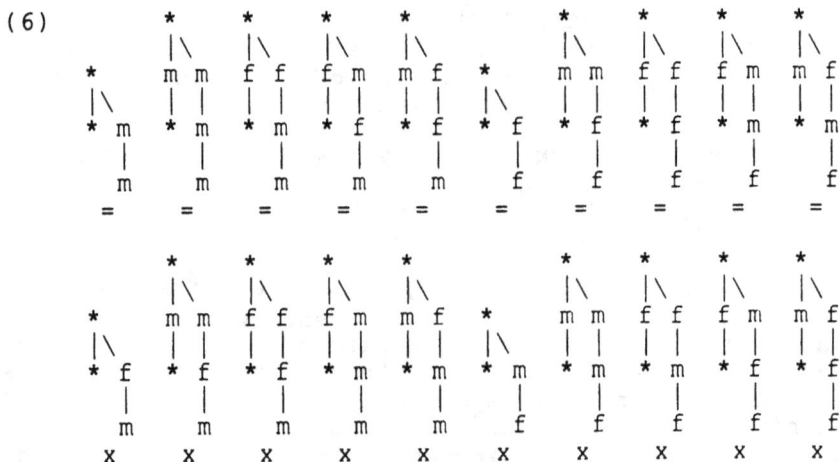

therefore, siblings, are called 'mother's children'. Two terms, listed in (7), mark the sex of 'mother's sons' and 'mother's daughters', respectively.

(7) paco macã (v)   =PfCm(G)   mother's son
     paco macõ (v)   =PfCf(G)   mother's daughter

Most Tucano kinsmen are related to one another in several ways, due to cross-cousin marriage. Whenever this is the case, the kinship terms for the closest relationship are used, and other more distant relationships are ignored. This being so, the two terms for 'parallel cousins' can be listed as in (7), with

the proviso that agnatic cousins rank as `siblings´
and are never considered to be `cousins´.

In particular, most individuals who are a moth-
er´s child (PfC) are also a father´s child (PmC) in
respect to ego, either because the father of the child
is ego´s own real father, or because he is a Tucano
and, thereby, a classificatory father. In the case,
however, of a woman who has children by two men--one a
Tucano, the other not--, the children are not `sib-
lings´; they are `mother´s children´ to one another.

The two terms of (7) extend by Rule G to all
parallel cousins who do not classify as agnatic
kinsmen. Figure (8) presents twelve possible parallel
cousin dyads for two degrees of collateral distance.
Of these dyads, the first two are agnatic (marked T
for Tucano) and fall within the range of `sibling´
terms. The remaining ten are nonagnatic and fall
within the range of the two `mother´s child´ terms.

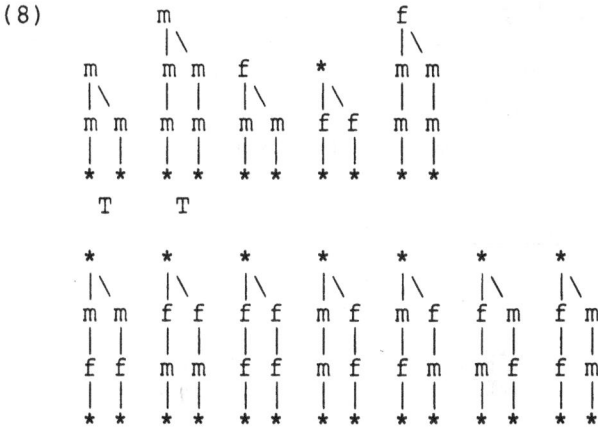

```
(8)           m                   f
              |\                  |\
      m     m m   f      *      m m
      |\    | |   |\     |\     | |
      m m   m m   m m   f f    m m
      | |   | |   | |   | |    | |
      * *   * *   * *   * *    * *
       T     T

      *     *     *     *     *     *     *
      |\    |\    |\    |\    |\    |\    |\
      m m   f f   f f   m f   m f   f m   f m
      | |   | |   | |   | |   | |   | |   | |
      f f   m m   f f   m f   f m   m f   f m
      | |   | |   | |   | |   | |   | |   | |
      * *   * *   * *   * *   * *   * *   * *
```

All classificatory `mother´s children´ are the
children of real or classificatory mother´s sisters or
of classificatory nonagnatic father´s brothers. They
are distinguished from classificatory siblings, who
are the children of classificatory agnatic or real
father´s brothers.

Cross cousins. Two terms, listed in (9), mark the
sex of cross cousins.

(9) basucʉ (meocã̃)   xPPCCm(G)   male cross cousin
     basuco (meocõ)   xPPCCf(G) female cross cousin

Any cross kinsman of ego's generation, whether linked through father or mother, is referred to by one of the two terms in (9), unless he is also linked as a 'sibling' or a 'mother's child', in which case either of these closer relationships takes precedence. Cross cousins are the children of real or classificatory mother's brothers, father's sisters, or both.

Paternal kinsmen. Paternal kinsmen are the male parallel kinsmen of the first ascending and descending generations and corresponding female cross kinsmen, as defined above in (5) and (6). There are three reciprocal sets of paternal kinsman terms.

One set of two terms, listed in (10), is used between a real or classificatory father's brother--the male parallel kintypes of (5) with male ego--and his real or classificatory fraternal sibling's son--the male parallel kintypes of (6) with male ego. The symbol 'M' in (10) represents the paternal or fraternal limitation on the defining PC strings.

(10) mee   (v)   MmPPCm(G)   man's paternal uncle
     meecã̃ (v)   MmPCCm(G)   man's fraternal nephew

A second set of two terms, listed in (11), is used between father's brother of female ego and a man's fraternal sibling's daughter--the male parallel kintypes of (5) with female ego and the female parallel kintypes of (6) with male ego.

(11) mʉgã̃ (v)   MfPPCm(G)   woman's paternal uncle
     macõ (v)   MmPCCf(G)   man's fraternal niece

The term for a man's fraternal niece is the daughter term presented above in (2), and represents, therefore, a disjunctive, extended sense of that term.

The third set of terms, listed in (12), consists of three terms. Together they are used between a real or classificatory father's sister--the female cross kintypes of (5) and corresponding more distantly related ones--and her real or classificatory fraternal sibling's child--the cross kintypes of (6) with female ego and corresponding more distantly related kintypes.

(12) wameo (v)   MPPCf(G)   paternal aunt
     parãmacã (v)   MfPCCm(G) woman's fraternal nephew
     parãmacõ (v)   MfPCCf(G) woman's fraternal niece

Maternal kinsmen. Maternal kinsmen in Tucano are
the male cross kinsmen and the female parallel kinsmen
of the first ascending generation. There are no
kinship terms for the corresponding kinsmen of the
first descending generation, these kinsmen being
referred to by descriptive phrases only.

There are three terms, listed in (13), for maternal kinsmen. Two terms, marking sex of ego, designate
maternal uncles, while a single term, disregarding the
sex of ego, designates maternal aunts. The symbol 'F'
in (13) represents the maternal limitation in the
defining PC strings.

(13) mecã   (v)   FmPPCm(G)   man's maternal uncle
     mecãsã (v)   FfPPCm(G)   woman's maternal uncle
     mugõ   (v)   FPPCf(G)   maternal aunt

Persons of the first descending generation who
use the terms in (13) are referred to reciprocally, as
mentioned above, by descriptive phrases. The phrases
are based on the sibling or cousin terms the maternal
kinsman would use for the junior kinsman's parent,
with either macã 'son' or macõ 'daughter' postposed in
a genitive construction. A few examples are listed in
(14).

(14) ma'mio macã   older sister's son
     basucu macõ   male cross cousin's daughter
     paco macõ macã   parallel cousin's son

In the case of a younger sister's daughter, male
ego uses a contracted form of the phrase used by
female ego, as indicated in (15).

(15) acabijo macã   woman's younger sister's son
     cabiocjã   man's younger sister's son
     acabijo macõ   woman's younger sister's daughter
     cabiocjõ   man's younger sister's daughter

Apart from these phrases, however, there is a
pair of terms listed in (16) which names the children
of a man's cross cousin. Such a child is the potential
spouse of ego's own child.

(16) paacꞪ (tiicjꞪ)   xmPPCCmCm(G)
                            man's male cross cousin's son
     paacõ (tiicjõ)   xmPPCCmCf(G)
                            man's male cross cousin's daughter

Kinsmen-in-law. There are just eight elementary
kinsman-in-law terms. Three terms, listed in (17),
name a spouse's father, a spouse's mother, and a
daughter's husband, respectively. The majority of such
kinsmen are maternal uncles (mecꞪ, mecꞪsã), paternal
aunts (wameo), and their reciprocals, as well as
kinsmen-in-law.

(17) mañecꞪ   SPm   father-in-law
     mañecõ   SPf   mother-in-law
     buji   CSm   son-in-law

A daughter-in-law is referred to descriptively as
'my son's wife' (yʉ'ʉ macꞪ nʉmo).

Four terms, listed in (18), mark the sex of ego
and alter for siblings-in-law, both the sibling of
spouse and the spouse of sibling (Rule V inversion).

(18) pe'ñʉ   mSPCm(V,Gm)   man's brother-in-law
     siõ   fSPCf(V,Gm)   woman's sister-in-law
     bujiba'cʉ   fSPCm(V,Gm)   woman's brother-in-law
     bujiba'co   mSPCf(V,Gm)   man's sister-in-law

A fifth term, listed in (19), designates a same-
sex co-sibling-in-law, the spouses of two same-sex
siblings.

(19) pe'su   aSPCSa(Gm) same-sex co-sibling-in-law

Spouses. There are two terms for husband and
wife, listed in (20).

(20) marꞪpʉ   Sm   husband
     nʉmo   Sf   wife

Vocative terms

Grandkinsmen. Bifurcate categories and phratry
affiliation are ignored in reference to grandkinsmen,
but are marked in direct address by eight vocative
terms, twice the number used in reference. The lineal
and first-degree collateral kintype dyads over which
these terms range are presented in (21), as an aid to

the following discussion. The dyads are grouped into three sets. The first dyad in each set is marked `M´ to indicate that the relationship is agnatic--ego and alter are both Tucano. The second dyad in each set is marked `F´ to indicate that the relationship is cognatic--the senior member of the dyad is a member of the junior member´s mother´s phratry. The third dyad in each set is marked `O´ meaning `other than the above´. The first set of dyads represent lineal kinsmen. The second set is marked `=´ to indicate parallel collaterals; the third set is marked `x´ to indicate cross kinsmen.2

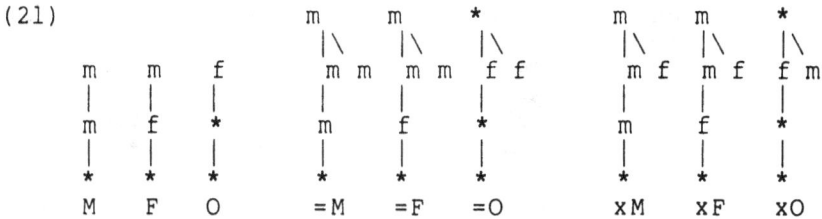

```
(21)                        m    m     *        m    m     *
                            |\   |\   |\        |\   |\   |\
      m    m    f         m m  m m   f f       m f  m f  f m
      |    |    |          |    |     |         |    |    |
      m    f    *          m    f     *         m    f    *
      |    |    |          |    |     |         |    |    |
      *    *    *          *    *     *         *    *    *
      M    F    O         =M   =F    =O        xM   xF   xO
```

There are two grandfather and two grandmother terms, listed in (22). The diagnostic features here are (1) whether the kinsman is male or female, and (2) whether he is Tucano, which is to say, agnatic, or not. Note that male agnates in this category are lineal (M) or parallel (=M), whereas corresponding females are cross (xM). Nonagnates are cognates (F) or others (O), without respect to bifurcate categories.

(22) pacɐjo   MPPm(Gm,S)   Tucano grandfather
     wameocjo   MPPf(Gm,S)   Tucano grandmother
     ñecɐjo   ⁻MPPm(G,S) non-Tucano grandfather
     ma´acjo   ⁻MPPf(G,S) non-Tucano grandmother

In the second descending generation, bifurcate categories are diagnostic rather than phratry affiliation, as the four terms in (23) show.

(23) macɐcjɐ   =mCCm(Gm,S)   man´s parallel grandson
     macɐcjõ   =mCCf(Gm,S) man´s parallel granddaughter
     pãrãmi   =fCCm,xCCm(Gm,S)   cross grandson
     pãrãmeo   =fCCf,xCCf(Gm,S)   cross granddaughter

Male ego has two terms which he uses for his lineal or parallel grandchildren whether they are Tucano or not. The second two terms are identical in form to those used in reference for any grandchild,

cross or parallel, as indicated above in (1). In
direct address, however, only a woman uses them for
the lineal grandchild of her opposite-sex ‘sibling‘.3

   Kinsmen-in-law. As indicated in (17) above, there
are special reference terms for parents- and children-
in-law, making specific reference to their affinal
relationship as opposed to any filial relationship
they may also have with ego. In direct address, filial
terms, listed in (24), are used. These are the same as
the reference terms presented above in (12) and (13).

(24) wameo   SPf   mother-in-law
      pãrữmacữ   fCSm   woman's son-in-law
      pãrữmacõ   fCSm   woman's daughter-in-law
      mecữ   mSPm   man's father-in-law
      mecữsã   fSPm   woman's father-in-law
      tiicjữ   mCSm   man's son-in-law
      tiicjõ   mCSf   man's daughter-in-law

   Siblings-in-law are typically cross cousins, and
the vocative forms, listed above in (9), function for
such kinsmen in direct address, as indicated in (25).

(25) meocữ   SPCm(V,Gm)   brother-in-law
      meocõ   SPCf(V,Gm)   sister-in-law

Tucano sibs

   According to our Tucano consultant, Dionisio
Cordero, all sibs of the Tucano phratry emerged from
the same rapids called Panure (Tjõpaduri in Tucano),
which are located on the Vaupés River below Yavarate.
Dionisio belongs to the sixth sib (Ne'rã Põ'rã),
listed in order below in (26), and says that his sib
Grandfather was named Yo puri oa capea. As indicated
previously, three kinship terms are assigned to these
sibs: grandfather (ñecữ), elder brother (ma'mi), and
younger brother (acabiji).

   Dionisio and his wife were able to supply the
names of twenty-six Tucano sibs, along with their
order of rank, the present location of most of them,
and the kinship term ranking his sib uses in respect
to each of them. This information is presented in
(26), with the grandfather, elder brother, and younger
brother sibs marked 1, 2, and 3, respectively. Sib
names marked by asterisk (*) are alternate names used
by the members of the particular sib themselves when

it is distinct from the name used by members of Dionisio's sib. When the Spanish name of a sib location is unknown, the Tucano name is listed. Communities located in Brazil are marked `B´ in the last column.

(26) **Tucano sibs:**

rank	name	kin	location	river
1	wa´uro põ´rã	2	Piracuara	Papuri
2	cuisere põ´rã	2	Piracuara	Papuri
3	maacupi põ´rã	2	Piracuara	Papuri
4	oye põ´rã	2	Patu	Papuri
5	ñaquẽ põ´rã	2	Montfort	Papuri
6	ne´rã põ´rã	-	Acaricuara	Paca
7	ñajuri põ´rã	3	Tamacuari	Papuri
8	mimisipe põ´rã	3	Arara	Paca
			Santa María	Papuri
9	ducu tẽrã	3	Tarira	Paca
10	buru põ´rã	3	above Mitú	Vaupés
11	sa´curo põ´rã	3	Montfort	Papuri
	*yaitaro põ´rã			
12	ba´ti tororã	3	Pari siripa	Tiquié B
13	sararo põ´rã	3	Acaricuara	Paca
	*ũrẽmirĩ		Guadalajara	Paca
14	di´ipe põ´rã	3	?	Tiquié B
15	turo põ´rã	3	Buena Vista	Tiquié B
16	o´me peri põ´rã	3	Guayapisuna	Papuri B
17	papera põ´rã	3	Yuyuta	Tiquié B
18	yu´ãrã	3	Melo Franco	Papuri B
19	bosoa	1	Carurú	Tiquié B
20	cu´marõ põ´rã	1	Santa Lucía	Papuri B
	*cã´rẽ põ´rã		San Miguél	
			Puerto Limón	Paca
21	baya põ´rã	1	Imisa poca	Papuri B
22	apũ queria	1	Omari	Vaupés B
23	cõjã pa põ´rã	3	?	Vaupés B
24	caperia	3	?	Vaupés B
25	ñirape põ´rã	1	Taracua	Vaupés B
			Sẽrãñoa	Vaupés B
26	bu´pua põ´rã	1	?	Vaupés B

The foregoing discussion has indicated how the Tucano people relate to one another within and between Tucano sibs. A further matter that still needs to be clarified in future study is the relationship of the Tucano people to members of other phratries--often isomorphic with linguistic communities, but not always. We know, for example, that the Bará and Barasano are considered to have some sort of sibling relationship with the Tucano, so that Tucanos do not marry with these two groups. Other linguistic communities with which the Tucano marry apparently stand in a cross-cousin relationship. Our language consultant, Dionisio, suggests that the Tucano originally preferred to marry Tuyucas, Desanas, Sirianas, and Tarianas, but that that preference seems to be waning. He also says that geographic proximity is a factor, but that incest taboos are still strictly adhered to. It has been observed that violation of the incest taboo results in isolation, especially of the female spouse when she is brought into her husband's home community to live.

NOTES

1

These data were gathered as part of a long-term research project of the Summer Institute of Linguistics begun in 1963 under the direction of Birdie West and Betty Welch. This study was undertaken by Marie Goehner, literacy consultant to the team, with the assistance of Birdie West, at an anthropology consultation directed by William R. Merrifield for SIL colleagues at Lomalinda, Meta, during February, 1983. Special thanks are due the helpful assistance of Dionisio Cordero, of the Tucano sib Ñe´rã Põ´rã, and his wife María, a fluent Tucano speaker whose father was Tuyuco and mother Tucana.

The orthography used for Tucano words is that used in literature prepared for Tucanos. Based on a phonological analysis, it has been adapted in part to Spanish orthographic conventions: c and qu for /k/; m, n, and ñ for /b d y/ in nasal syllables; and j for /h/. A tilde (~) marks nasalization when not otherwise marked by m, n, or ñ. ʉ is /ɨ/; apostrophe (´) stands for glottal closure. See West and Welch (1967) for details concerning Tucano phonology.

2

The definitions of 'parallel' and 'cross' presented earlier in the paper for kinsmen less than two generations removed from ego do not cover kintypes of the second generation from ego, but we have not modified them for the simple reason that our analysis to date does not go beyond one degree of collateral distance for these generations. Suffice it so say, for the moment, that neither sex of ego's parent nor sex of alter's parent is counted in the dyads of (21).

3
This disjunction can be stated formally as follows:

$$= \ \text{-->} \ x \ / \ fCC,$$

which may be read:

"for female ego, a parallel grandchild is terminologically equivalent to a cross grandchild."

REFERENCES

Fields, Harriet L. and William R. Merrifield. 1980. Mayoruna (Panoan) kinship. Ethnology 19:1-28.

Sorenson, Arthur P., Jr. 1967. Multilingualism in the Northwest Amazon. American Anthropologist 69:670-84.

West, Birdie and Betty Welch. 1967. Phonemic system of Tucano. In Phonemic systems of Colombian languages 1:11-24. Norman: Summer Institute of Linguistics of the University of Oklahoma.

GUAHIBO KINSHIP TERMINOLOGY

William R. Merrifield & Riena Kondo
Summer Institute of Linguistics, Dallas & Colombia

A number of excellent studies of Guahibo kinship terminology have appeared in recent years (Wilbert 1957, Morey and Morey 1974, Queixalos 1980) so that this one will move swiftly over old ground and focus upon differences of comparative interest within a language group with several dialect areas (Kondo 1982) as well as contribute new data in respect to one or two areas of the terminological system.1

The most significant new knowledge which this treatment reveals is that the Guahibo terminology is not Iroquois, but is of a standard Dravidian type, which defines the bifurcate categories `parallel` and `cross` in the manner of many aboriginal systems of Australia of which Kariera (Romney and Epling 1958) is a well-known example. Lounsbury (1964:1079) has clarified the difference between Iroquois systems--which calculate bifurcate categories on the basis of the relative sex of just two kinsmen in the genealogical chain which links ego to alter--and Dravidian systems--which take into account the sex of all such linking kinsmen.

The specific characteristics of the Kariera subtype have been briefly discussed by Fields and Merrifield (1980:17) in a discussion of the Mayoruna subtype which varies only slightly from it. Now it can be said that both Kariera and Mayoruna subtypes as well as a third, the Suruí type, are in use by indigenous peoples of Colombia. The Suruí (Brazil) type (Bontkes and Merrifield 1985) is shared by the Cubeo (Morse 1985), the Mayoruna (Peru) type by Tucano (Goehner, West, and Merrifield 1985), and now the Kariera type by Guahibo.

The basic principle underlying bifurcate categories of Kariera, Mayoruna, and Guahibo is the same,

71

and is stated in (1).

(1)   PARALLEL (GUAHIBO): Within the genealogical chain
      that links ego to alter, there are an even
      $(0,2,4,...,n)$ number of male kinsmen and an even
      number of female kinsmen.

      CROSS (GUAHIBO): Within the genealogical chain
      that links ego to alter, there are an odd
      $(1,3,5,...,n)$ number of male kinsmen and an odd
      number of female kinsmen.

The specific characteristic which distinguishes
Guahibo and Kariera from Mayoruna (and Tucano) is in
the definition of which kinsmen in the genealogical
chain linking ego to alter are 'counted' in the above
calculation. For Guahibo, the sex of ego is only
relevant to the determination of the bifurcate category of a kinsman of the first descending generation.
Conversely, the sex of alter is only diagnostic of the
bifurcate category of a kinsman of the first ascending
generation. Otherwise, the sex of all linking kinsmen
must be taken into account except that of the common
ancestor(s) of ego and alter.

The following presentation focusses principally
upon the terms of reference. There are only minor
differences in linguistic notation from that of
previous studies--primarily in the marking of details
of vowel length--some of which may represent dialectal
variation. Unless otherwise indicated, the terms
presented in this paper are as spoken at Caño Jabón on
the Guaviare River in the Department of Meta,
Colombia. The other dialect referred to here is spoken
along the Vichada River near San José de Ocuné,
Vichada Territory (Comisaría). Terms in parentheses
following those from Caño Jabón are variants as spoken
near San José. Most of them differ only by length
contrasts.

Grandkinsmen

Bifurcate categories are not marked for grandkinsmen. Just four terms, listed in (1), mark sex and
seniority of all filial kinsmen beyond the first
ascending and the first descending generations (Rule
1). They further extend to all corresponding stepkinsmen and kinsmen-in-law (in the sense of Lounsbury
1965), as well as to stepkinsmen-in-law, by Rule S,
which for Guahibo is to be interpreted as adding the

Spouse relation (S) to the beginning, end, or both beginning and end of any primary or extended filial PC string.

(1) a<u>mo</u> (amo)	PPm(1,S)	grandfather
<u>a</u>cue (acue)	PPf(1,S)	grandmother
mo<u>mo</u>	CCm(1,S)	grandson
mom<u>oyo</u>	CCf(1,S)	granddaughter

Morey and Morey found a self-reciprocal term (ewan<u>i</u>) for grandparents and grandchildren of three or more generations´ distance from ego. This term is unknown in the San José de Ocuné or Caño Jabón dialects. Caño Jabón has two terms, listed in (2), for such kinsmen.

| (2) <u>o</u>rov<u>e</u> | PPP(1,S) | great-grandparent |
| n<u>ave</u> | CCC(1,S) | great-grandchild |

Affinal extension of these and other Guahibo terms is intimately related to a strong preference for bilateral cross-cousin marriage and sister exchange. The chicken-and-egg question has not been entirely resolved in this regard for Guahibo, in that because of the commonness of multiple relationships between any two kinsmen due to extensive intermarriage, we have not been able to satisfy ourselves to date that such affinal extension of terms is in fact independent of actual filial ties through other lines of reckoning. It is our present belief, however, that the ubiquity of cross-cousin marriage and the compatibility of the system with such marriages has resulted in affinal extension which would be unquestioned even in the absence of an appropriate filial tie between affinal kinsmen.

Parent and child generations

Terms for kinsmen of the first ascending and first descending generations fall into three sets of four--lineal, parallel, and cross--each marking only sex of kinsman and seniority.

Lineal terms, listed in (3), have only primary denotations, except that in the case of very small children, they may extend to stepkinsmen. When children grow up, they tend to switch to the use of terms for parallel kinsmen, listed in (4), in reference to stepkinsmen.

(3) apa (axa)   Pm(-S)   father
     ena (ena)   Pf(-S)   mother
     xɨnato   Cm(S-)   son
     xɨnatoyo   Cf(S-)   daughter

(4) axuanɨ   =PPCm(G,S)   parallel uncle
     enava   =PPCf(G,S)   parallel aunt
     jianɨ   =PCCm(G,S)   parallel nephew
     jianɨyo   =PCCf(G,S)   parallel niece

The kintype dyads over which the parallel terms
range are illustrated in (5), for two degrees of
collaterality. The two terms for senior parallel kinsmen name the kinsmen of appropriate sex which correspond to the right terminus of each dyad, while the
terms for junior kinsmen name those which correspond
to their left termini.

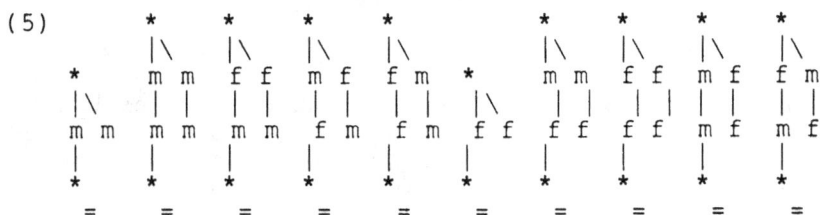

(5)
```
        *     *     *     *        *     *     *     *
        |\    |\    |\    |\       |\    |\    |\    |\
  *     m m   f f   m f   f m  *   m m   f f   m f   f m
  |\    | |   | |   | |   | |   |\  | |   | |   | |   | |
  m m   m m   m m   f m   f m   f f f f   f f   m f   m f
  |     |     |     |     |     |   |     |     |     |
  *     *     *     *     *     *   *     *     *     *

  =     =     =     =     =     =   =     =     =     =
```

Since, by definition, spouses are of the opposite
sex, the extension of terms for parallel kinsmen to
corresponding affinals in the context of bilateral
cross-cousin marriage is like throwing a toggle switch
in calculating bifurcate categories. The parallel
kinsman terms of (4), therefore, extend to the spouse
of cross kinsman or to the cross kinsman of spouse. In
the case of stepkinsman-in-law, the 'toggle' is effec-
tively thrown twice so that the terms of (4) apply to
the spouses of spouse's parallel kinsmen of the first
ascending and first descending generations.

The terms for cross kinsmen of the parent and
child generations are listed in (6).

(6) axu (axuyo)   xPPCm(G,S)   cross uncle
     ame (ame)   xPPCf(G,S)   cross aunt
     opaxa   xPCCm(G,S)   cross nephew
     ecopenayo   xPCCf(G,S)   cross niece

The kintype dyads which correspond to the first
two degrees of collateral extension of the terms in

(6) are graphically displayed in (7), and should be read in the same manner as for the terms for parallel kinsmen. Affinal extension also has the same effect, in reverse, as for the parallel terms. Kinsmen-in-law of the parent and child generations are classified by these cross-kinsmen terms, whether or not the filial relationship exists, although in the majority of cases it does.

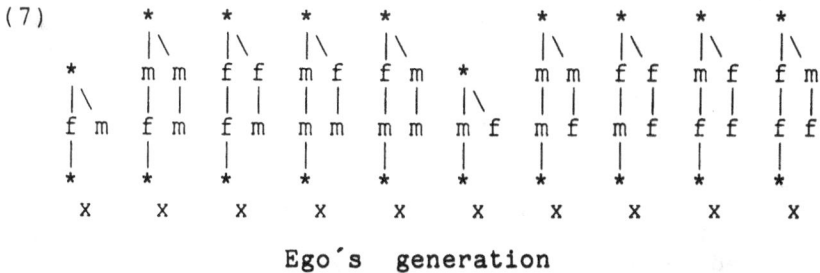

```
(7)         *      *      *      *          *      *      *      *
           |\     |\     |\     |\         |\     |\     |\     |\
     *      m m    f f    m f    f m    *    m m    f f    m f    f m
    |\     | |    | |    | |    | |    |\   | |    | |    | |    | |
    f m    f m    f m    f m    m m    m m  m f    m f    m f    f f    f f
    |      |      |      |      |      |    |      |      |      |
    *      *      *      *      *      *    *      *      *      *

    x      x      x      x      x      x    x      x      x      x
```

Ego's generation

Kinsmen of ego's generation are parallel or cross. Four terms, listed in (8), designate siblings in their primary senses, marking sex and seniority. The alternate terms for siblings (ato and ova) are used in reference and address in Caño Jabón, but are only heard vocatively and without pronouns in San José de Ocuné.2 The terms found in Morey and Morey (1974) for younger siblings (ewato and metayo) are not found in San José or Caño Jabón.

(8) matapijini̱, ato̱   =ePCm(G,S)   elder brother
    matapijiva̱, ova̱   =ePCf(G,S)   elder sister
    juyapijini̱   =yPCm(G,S)   younger brother
    juyapijiva̱   =yPCf(G,S)   younger sister

The sibling terms extend filially, by Rule G, to the parallel kinsmen of ego's generation, the children of kinsmen referred to by the parallel aunt and uncle terms listed in (4) and represented graphically in (5). Sibling terms extend affinally, by Rule S and with the 'toggle' effect mentioned above, to the spouses of cross cousins, to the cross cousins of spouse, and to spouse's siblings' spouses.

Unlike some other language communities of Colombia, seniority of siblings is always calculated directly in Guahibo on the basis of the relative age of ego and alter, even in extended senses of sibling terms. By way of contrast, Cubeo (Morse 1984), and

Tucano (Goehner, West, and Merrifield 1984) calculate seniority only on the basis of the true siblings within the chain that links more distant ones.

The terms for cross cousins are listed in (9). These terms mark the sex of both ego and alter.

(9) amojo, nerimani̱   xmPCm(G,S)   man's male cousin
    amojova̱, nerīva̱   xfPCf(G,S) woman's female cousin
    banani̱   xfPCm(G,S)   woman's male cousin
    banava̱   xmPCf(G,S)   man's female cousin
    cotiva̱   xaPCb(G,S)   opposite-sex cousin

Cross cousins of the the same sex can apparently choose freely between two terms for these relationships, as indicated in (9). The second term for a woman's female cousin has the form nerimava̱ in San José, with the syllables ima corresponding to the nasalized ī of the Caño Jabón term. The last term in (9) is used for an opposite-sex cousin, but is less polite than the two terms above it and is never used in the presence of the person referred to.

Cross cousins are the children of the first ascending generation cross kinsmen named in (6) and represented graphically in (7). In the nature of the case, the primary range of cross cousin terms is at two degrees of collateral distance (in contrast to sibling terms). Cross-cousin terms extend affinally to the spouses of siblings, the siblings of spouse, and to spouse's cross-cousins' spouses.

Spouses

Spouse is ideally a cross cousin of the opposite sex, and is referred to after marriage by one of the terms listed in (10).

(10) amono (amona)   Sm   husband
     va̱   Sf   wife

Greetings

The dialect of Guahibo spoken near San José de Ocuné has a feature not mentioned in Morey and Morey (1974), namely, a variation in the form of terms when used as a greeting, distinct from their regular use in direct address. In greeting a person, this special form of a term is used, acknowledging the presence of

the kinsman but without further verbal interaction
with him. Greeting forms differ from regular vocatives
by vowel length. Thus, ame is the regular vocative for
`mother-in-law´, but ame is the corresponding greeting
term. In Caño Jabón, greetings are identical to vocative forms except for intonation. Vocatives end with
high pitch, greetings with low pitch. This is also
true of the terms in San José.

Women use greeting forms for both male and female
kinsmen. Men use them only for greeting females. To
greet a male, a man always approaches him and speaks
directly to him, using a vocative form of the appropriate kinship term.

NOTES

1
This study is part of a long-range project of
the Summer Institute of Linguistics directed by Victor
and Riena Kondo, who have been studying Guahibo
language and culture since 1963, first at Barranco
Colorado on the Meta River near Orocué (5 years), and
then at Corocito on the Vichada River near San José de
Ocuné. Data from Caño Jabón were provided by Luis
Alberto Rodríguez.

Guahibo forms are written in an orthography
adapted to Spanish for Guahibo readers: c and qu
represent /k/; j represents /h/. x is /x/, ɨ is a high
back unround vowel, tilde (˜) is nasalization, and
long vowels are underlined. See Kondo (1984) for
further details regarding the sounds of Guahibo.

2
Except for a few vocative terms, Guahibo kinship
terms occur with pronominal prefixes (Kondo 1975)
which vary somewhat in form between dialects.

REFERENCES

Bontkes, Carolyn & William R. Merrifield. 1985. On
Suruí (Tupian) social organization. This volume.

Fields, Harriet L. and William R. Merrifield. 1980.
Mayoruna (Panoan) kinship. Ethnology 19:1-28.

Goehner, Marie, Birdie West, and William R. Merrifield. 1985. Tucano (Tucanoan) kinship terminology. This volume.

Kondo, Riena W. de. 1982. La familia lingüística guahiba. Artículos en lingüistica y campos afines 11:37-75. Lomalinda: Instituto Lingüístico de Verano.

-----. 1984. Contribución al estudio de longitud vocálica y acento en el idioma guahibo. Artículos en lingüistica y campos afines 13. In press.

Kondo, Victor. 1975. A tagmemic description of Guahibo (sentence to morpheme). Lomalinda: Summer Institute of Linguistics. 139 pp.

Lounsbury, Floyd G. 1964. The structural analysis of kinship semantics. In H. G. Lunt (ed.), Proceedings of the ninth international congress of linguists, 1073-93. The Hague: Mouton and Co.

-----. 1965. Another view of the Trobriand kinship categories. In E. A. Hammel (ed.), Formal semantic analysis. American anthropologist 67:5 (part 2):142-85.

Morey, Robert V. and Nancy C. Morey. 1974. Terminología del parentesco guahibo. Revista Colombiana de Antropología 16:249-58.

Morse, Nancy. 1985. Cubeo (Tucanoan) kinship terminology. This volume.

Queixalos, F. 1980. Contribución al estudio del parentesco sikwani (guahibo): un enfoque lingüístico. Antropológicas 2:89-104. Bogotá: Sociedad Antropológica de Colombia.

Romney, A. K. and P. J. Epling. 1958. A simplified model of Kariera kinship. American anthropologist 60:59-74.

Wilbert, J. 1957. Notes on Guahibo kinship and social organization. Southwestern journal of anthropology 13:88-98.

CUBEO KINSHIP

Nancy L. Morse
Summer Institute of Linguistics, Colombia

The purpose of this paper is to present the phratry organization and the kinship terms of refer- ence and address with their ranges of extension of the Cubeo people of southeastern Colombia as used today by at least five of the sibs living on the four main rivers of the Cubeo territory.1

I have been greatly helped in my understanding of the Cubeo culture by Goldman's work, but realized that the Cubeos I live with use kinship terms not included in his list (1963:134).

Cubeo words in this paper are written in an orthography designed by those who did the phonological analysis (Salser and Salser 1976) which takes into consideration facility of transfer between Cubeo and Spanish. The following orthographic symbols are different from Spanish: ´ (stress, marked only when it falls on other than the second syllable of a word), ~ (nasalization), ʉ /ɨ/, and đ /đ/. Other Cubeo symbols are comparable to corresponding ones of Spanish.

The Cubeo call themselves and other indigenous people pãmiwã. Other named language groups of their area are the Guanano (ocoyʉwa), the Carapana (mʉrẽwã), the Yurutí (juređariwa), the Tucano (joewewa), the Curripaco (macapõewã), the Siriano (pʉimiwã), the Desano (´wecuiwa), the Barasano (pididapãrãmena), the Tuyuca (jorobođapãrãmena), the Tatuyo (pãmuwã), the Piratapuyo (moapãrãmena), and the Cacua (borowa). Nonindigenous people are ñarãdawiwa, literally `wealthy ones´. People are also referred to as `ones from such-and-such a place´, for example, the Brazil- ians (duicacawʉ), the Peruvians (perucawʉ), and the Venezuelans (benechu´eracawʉ). Among the Cubeos them- selves a person's consanguines are ´jiwʉ, literally `my ones´. A person's in-laws are ´jicoyʉmarã, literally `the people to whom I speak'. People who are not affines or consanguines are apewʉ, `other ones'. Another unrelated indigenous person is addressed as majẽcʉ (masculine), majẽco (feminine), or majẽwʉ (plural).

Phratries and sibs

The study of Cubeo phratries and sibs is closely related to the study of kinship in that an individual must know how sibs are grouped into phratries in order to know who are eligible spouses, and one must know the rank order of the sibs in order to know to whom to refer and address as `elder sibling' or as `younger sibling'.

Goldman has stated (1963:90) that

> The Cubeo sib is a unilineal descent group whose members regard themselves as being descended from common ancestors but cannot establish an actual genealogical relationship. Sibs are named, normally localized, exogamic, patrilineal, and patrilocal. They are bound into unnamed exogamic phratries within which they occupy an order of rank that expresses the sequence in which they emerged during their mythical first emergence. Sib members claim descent from the male of an ancestral brother-sister pair. Each sib bears a name that in some cases is the name of the sib founder, but in any case is the name of an Ancient, that is, an early ancestor.

Such a founder is called bʉcʉpõecʉ (masculine), bʉcʉpõeco (feminine), or bʉcʉpõewã (plural).

Presently the Cubeos recognize twelve sibs, comprising the first two phratries of Table 1, as `true Cubeos' (pãmiwã). A third phratry of six sibs speaks Cubeo, but is considered to be `other people' (apewʉ). The subsibs mentioned by Goldman (1963:100-105) are not distinguished by the Cubeos I know.

Phratries, as such, are not ranked; but sibs are listed in rank order in Table 1 following Goldman's numbering (1963:100-105), along with the origin site, river of origin, and the current location of each sib.

Table 1. Cubeo sibs.
==

Sib	Phratry	Origin-site	River	Locations
āuwewa	1	Santa Cruz	Vaupés	Vaupés/Cuduyarí
jejenawā	1	Santa Cruz	Vaupés	Vaupés/Cuduyarí
bajucᵾwa	1	Santa Cruz	Vaupés	Vaupés/Cuduyarí
pedicūwā	1	Barai	Cuduyarí	Cuduyarí
waɖariwa	1	Punto Ají	Vaupés	Vaupés
ijowedowa	1	Sudar	Cuduyarí	Cuduyarí
uchiwaiwa	1	Yuriparí	Vaupés	Vaupés/Cuduyarí
pia´rawa	1	Miraflores	Vaupés	Vaupés
mia´ɖāwā	2	Yuriparí	Vaupés	Vaupés
biowa	2	Santa Cruz	Vaupés	Querarí/Pirabotón
corowa	2	Santa Cruz	Vaupés	Querarí
jᵾrᵾwa	2	Santa Cruz	Vaupés	Cuduyarí
yᵾremawā	3	Aiyarí	Isana	Querarí
´yaniwā	3	Aiyarí	Isana	Querarí/Vaupés
yocacᵾbewᵾ	3	Aiyarí	Isana	Querarí
coɖēitarabᵾawᵾ	3	Aiyarí	Isana	Querarí
´torᵾawᵾ	3	Aiyarí	Isana	Querarí
betowa	3	Aiyarí	Isana	Querarí

As has been mentioned, the three phratries are exogamous. Each of the other previously mentioned language groups of the area can also be considered an exogamous phratry (cf. Waltz and Waltz 1982:6). A Cubeo may marry someone from any of these phratries other than his own, with the exception of the Cacua phratry.

A Cubeo calls members of his own phratry `elder sibling´ or `younger sibling´ depending on the order of emergence of their respective ancestors. In actual practice, because of the preference for bilateral cross-cousin marriage, there are usually members of only a few sibs in any given family. For example, three waɖariwa brothers married three Guanano women and their children have married Curripaco, Carapana, Guanano, coɖēitarabᵾawᵾ, mia´ɖāwā, and yᵾremawā spouses. Another example is of two jejenawā brothers, one of whom married a Yurutí and the other, a bioco. Their children have married biowa, mia´ɖāwā, ´yaniwā, and Yurutí spouses. A fuller statistically-based study of marriage patterns should be undertaken to provide further information on this subject.

The Cubeo kinship system

The Cubeo use a bifurcate system of kinship reference of the Dravidian type (Lounsbury 1964:1079), with `cross´ and `parallel´ defined as in the Suruí subtype (Bontkes and Merrifield 1985):

PARALLEL (Suruí): Within the genealogical chain that links ego to a designated kinsman, whenever there are two kinsmen of the same generation within the chain, those two kinsmen are of the same sex.

CROSS (Suruí): Within the genealogical chain that links ego to a designated kinsman, there is at least one pair of opposite-sex kinsmen of the same generation.

A graphic representation of parallel and cross kintype dyads for male kinsmen of the first ascending generation is given in (1).

Kinship terms are like other animate nouns in Cubeo which mark gender. Terms for male kinsmen generally have one of the masculine suffixes, -cʉ or -mʉ. Terms for kinswomen have one of the feminine suffixes, -co or -mo. Terms for male kinsmen which do not have one of these suffixes are either abbreviations, as

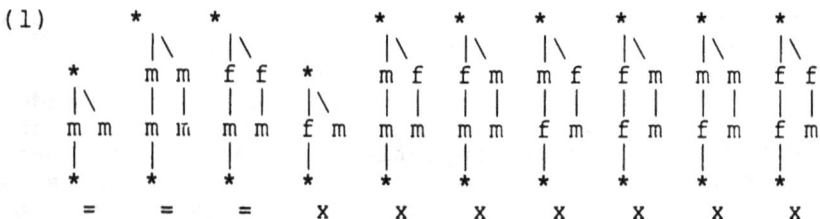

```
(1)        *    *           *     *     *     *     *     *
          |\   |\          |\    |\    |\    |\    |\    |\
    *     m m  f f    *     m f   f m   m f   f m   m m   f f
   |\     | |  | |   |\     | |   | |   | |   | |   | |   | |
   m m    m m  m m   f m    m m   m m   f m   f m   f m   f m
   |      |    |     |      |     |     |     |     |     |
   *      *    *     *      *     *     *     *     *     *
   =      =    =     x      x     x     x     x     x     x
```

with some vocative terms, or have the suffix -yo, which Goldman considers partitive (1963:119), and which may also be an honorific. All Cubeo kinship terms of reference are obligatorily possessed, and are here presented in their first person singular forms.

Terms of reference

Grandkinsman terms. Four grandkinsman terms extend collaterally, without respect to sib or phratry affiliation, to all kinsmen two or more generations distant from ego (Rule 1), and affinally (Rule S), which for Cubeo includes the spouses of grandkinsmen, the grandkinsmen of spouse, and the spouses of grand- kinsmen of spouse. Two terms distinguish the sex of grandparents and two distinguish the sex of grand- children, as listed in (2).

(2) ˈjiñecũyo   PPm(1,S)   grandfather
     ˈjiñeco   PPf(1,S)   grandmother
     jipãrãmecʉ   CCm(1,S)   grandson
     jipãrãmeco   CCf(1,S)   granddaughter

As Goldman (1963:126) has noted, "The ignoring of sib lines for grandparents seems to follow from the simple fact that at this generation level exogamy is not an issue." It probably also follows from the ambiguity which arises in distant generations in the presence of bilateral cross-cousin marriage and sister exchange, both practiced by the Cubeo, where all grandparents are related to ego, at least struc- turally, through both father and mother.

Parent and child terms. In parent and child gener- ations, four sets of terms distinguish lineal, lineal step, parallel, and cross kinsmen. The first set includes four terms which designate the lineal members of the nuclear family. Two of the terms distinguish the sex of parents and the other two distinguish the sex of children, as listed in (3).

(3) jipacʉ   Pm   father
     jipaco   Pf   mother
     ˈjimacʉ   Cm   son
     ˈjimaco   Cf   daughter

The second set includes four terms which desig- nate lineal stepkinsmen. Two of the terms distinguish the sex of stepparents and the other two distinguish the sex of stepchildren, as listed in (4).

(4) jipacoi ˈmarẽpacʉ   PSm   stepfather
     jipacʉi ˈmarẽpaco   PSf   stepmother
     ˈjibʉwaimʉ   SCm   stepson
     ˈjibʉwaimo   SCf   stepdaughter

The third set includes four terms which mark the sex of parallel kinsmen of the first ascending and the first descending generations. They extend collater- ally (Rule G) to all parentsʼ ʻsiblingsʼ and affinally to corresponding stepkinsmen--the spouses of ascending-generation collaterals and the descending-generation collaterals of spouse (Lounsbury 1965:163), as listed in (5).

(5) jipacᴜmacᴜ =PCm(G,-S)   father´s brother
    jipacomaco =PPCf(G,-S)   mother´s sister
    ñᴜjẽmacᴜ =PCCm(G,S-)   same-sex sibling´s son
    ñᴜjẽmaco =PCCf(G,S-) same-sex sibling´s daughter

The fourth set of terms includes six terms for cross kinsmen of the first ascending and first descending generations. Two terms distinguish the sex of kinsmen of the first ascending generation, and four distinguish the sex of both ego and his kinsman of the first descending generation. They extend collaterally (Rule G) to all cross kinsmen of these generations. These terms are listed in (6). Some speakers on the Vaupés River use jipārīmu for `mother´s brother´.

(6) jipārīyo   xPPCm(G,-S)   mother´s brother
    jipārīmo   xPPCf(G,-S)   father´s sister
    ´jiyᴜicᴜ   xmPCCm(G,S-)   man´s sister´s son
    ´jiyᴜico   xmPCCf(G,S-) man´s sister´s daughter
    jipārãmocᴜ xfPCCm(G,S-)   woman´s brother´s son
    jipārãmoco xfPCCf(G,S-) woman´s brother´s daughter

Sibling and cousin terms. Two sets of terms classify kinsmen of ego´s generation. In the first set, four terms rank siblings by relative age and mark their sex. These are listed in (7). In the case of true and step siblings, relative age of ego and alter is marked directly; in the case of more distant collaterals--the terms extend by Rule G--ranking is determined by the relative age of the true sibling pair in the chain which links ego to kinsman, that is, ego´s parent and the sibling of that parent in the case of a parallel first cousin, ego´s grandparent and the sibling of that grandparent in the case of a parallel second cousin, and so forth.

(7) jimamicᴜ   =ePCm(G)   elder brother
    jimamico   =ePCf(G)   elder sister
    ´jiyocᴜ   =yPCm(G)   younger brother
    ´jiyoco   =yPCf(G)   younger sister

In the second set, listed in (8), two terms distinguish the sex of cross cousins, and the terms are extended collaterally (Rule 1) to include all

cross kinsmen in ego's generation and descending generations. These terms designate potential spouses.

(8) ´jichimacʉ   xPPCCm(1)   male cross cousin
    ´jichimaco   xPPCCf(1)   female cross cousin

Spouse . terms. Two terms, inflected for sex,
designate actual spouses.

(9) ´jimarẽpacʉ   Sm   husband
    ´jimarẽpaco   Sf   wife

Kinsman-in-law terms. As indicated above, stepkinsmen are included within the extended ranges of
corresponding filial terms, with the exception of
lineal stepkinsmen; and grandkinsmen terms extend to
corresponding grandkinsmen-in-law and even to step-
grandkinsmen-in-law. This section presents four special sets of terms for the remaining kinsmen-in-law.

The first of these sets includes two self-reciprocal terms which designate parents- and children-in-
law. The first term designates both father-in-law and
son-in-law and the second, both mother-in-law and
daughter-in-law (Rule I). Both extend collaterally
(Rule G) and affinally to corresponding stepkinsmen-
in-law (Rule -S, which becomes S- when I is applied).
These are listed in (10).

(10) ´jiwacʉ   SPm(I,G,-S)   father/son-in-law
     ´jiwaco   SPf(I,G,-S) mother/daughter-in-law

The terms in (11) are alternates of those in
(10), but only for parents-in-law and stepparents-in-
law (Rule I does not apply). Note that these are not
new terms; they were listed above in (8) and are
filial terms which, because of a strong preference for
cross-cousin marriage and `sister´ exchange, result in
the mother's brother and the father's sister being
structurally equivalent to, if not actual, parents-in-
law.

(11) jipãrĩyo, jipãrĩmu SPm(G,-S)   father-in-law
     jipãrĩmo   SPf(G,-S)   mother-in-law

The . third set, listed in (12), includes four
terms for siblings-in-law, which include anyone called
`sibling´ by spouse and the spouse of anyone who calls

ego `sibling´ (Rules V and G), marking sex of both ego and kinsman.

(12) ´jicoy+m+   =mSPCm(V,G)   man´s brother-in-law
      ´jiwẽmo   =fSPCf(V,G)   woman´s sister-in-law
      ´jicapen+m+ =fSPCm(V,G)   woman´s brother-in-law
      ´jicapen+mo =mSPCf(V,G)   man´s sister-in-law

Finally, two terms, in (13), denote same-sex co-siblings-in-law. They extend collaterally (Rule G).

(13) ´jitebuc+   =mSPCSm(G)   co-brother-in-law
      ´jitebuco   =fSPCSf(G)   co-sister-in-law

Terms of address

The Cubeo kinship terms of address for cross cousins, stepchildren, and siblings-in-law are identical to the corresponding terms of reference. Other terms of address are phonologically similar to the corresponding terms of reference; often the only difference is that the reference term is possessed and there is a change in stress. There are fewer terms of address; some kinsmen who are distinguished by reference terms are classified together by vocative terms.

Grandkinsman terms. The two senior grandkinsman terms of address are the corresponding reference terms without the possessive prefix and with change of stress on the masculine term. The two junior grand-kinsman terms are very similar to the reference terms with the diminutive suffix -jĩ and without the pos-sessive prefix. The four terms extend collaterally (Rule 1) and affinally (Rule S), as do the correspond-ing reference terms. Each term designates the sex of kinsman as listed in (14).

(14) ñecũ´yo   PPm(1,S)   grandfather
      ñeco   PPf(1,S)   grandmother
      pãrãjĩc+   CCm(1,S)   grandson
      pãrãjĩco   CCf(1,S)   granddaughter

Parent and child terms. As in the case of the referential terminology, there are four pairs of voca-tive terms that distinguish lineal, lineal step, parallel, and cross senior kinsmen. The terms of address for the cross kinsmen are the corresponding reference terms without the possessive prefix and with change of stress. The other terms are phonologically similar to the corresponding terms of reference. The parallel and cross terms extend collaterally (Rule G) and affinally (Rule -S). One term of each pair desig- nates a male kinsman and the other a female kinsman, as listed in (15). Some speakers on the Vaupés River use pacɥ for `father´, and some speakers on the Querarí River use pai´yo, a vestige of Arawak. Ba is an abbreviated form of ´baco; both are used by all speakers.

(15) ´bayɥ, pacɥ, pai´yo   Pm   father
      ´baco, ba   Pf   mother
      yɥre bɥwayɥ   PSm   stepfather
      yɥre bɥwaɖo   PSf   stepmother
      pacɥ´yo   =PPCm(G,-S)   father´s brother
      paco   =PPCf(G,-S)   mother´s sister
      parī´yo   xPPCm(G,-S)   mother´s brother
      parī´mo   xPPCf(G,-S)   father´s sister

Three pairs of terms, listed in (16), distinguish kinsmen in the child generation. The first pair desig- nates filial kinsmen, lineal or collateral and with- out respect to bifurcate categories, of any descend- ing generation; the second pair designates lineal stepchildren; and the third pair designates nonlineal children and grandchildren. A further term denotes a junior kinsman without reference to sex. Some speakers on the Vaupés River also use this term for a younger sibling, in which case its range is defined as C(y2), where y2 indicates extension by Rule 2 (Merrifield 1983) with the limit that only kinsmen younger than ego are counted.

(16) bɥcɥ   Cm(1)   son
      bɥco   Cf(1)   daughter
      ´jibɥwaimɥ   SCm   stepson
      ´jibɥwaimo   SCf   stepdaughter
      jūai´yo   PCCm(G,S-)   nephew
      jūai´co   PCCf(G,S-)   niece
      bɥcɥrɥ   C(1)   child

Sibling and cousin terms. As in the case of the referential terminology, there are two sets of terms used in direct address which distinguish parallel kinsmen of ego´s generation from the corresponding cross kinsmen. The two sets together range over the same kintypes, as a whole, but do so by distinguishing slightly different factors.

In the case of siblings, sex of kinsman is distinguished for elder siblings, but not for younger
ones, as in (17). As with the corresponding reference
terms, these terms extend collaterally (Rule G).

(17) āmiˆyo   =ePCm(G)   elder brother
     āmiˆco   =ePCf(G)   elder sister
     buchu   =yPC(G)   younger sibling

In the case of cross cousins, male and female ego
have separate terms for male cousin, in vocative
usage, but not for female cousin, as in (18). As with
the corresponding reference terms, these terms extend
(Rule 1) to all cross kinsmen of egoˆs and descending
generations.

(18) chima   xmPPCCm(1)   manˆs male cross cousin
     ˆjichimacu   xfPPCCm(1)   womanˆs male cross cousin
     ˆjichimaco   xPPCCf(1)   female cross cousin

There is another pair of vocatives, but following
both Goldman (1963:134) and Salser (1965-71), I consider them terms of endearment rather than kinship
terms. They are chumi (masculine) and chumico (feminine). They are used by parents for children, by
uncles and aunts for nephews and nieces, and for any
younger sibling.

Kinsman-in-law terms. There are two sets of vocative terms for kinsmen-in-law. The first consists of
four terms which designate the sex of parents- and
children-in-law. They extend collaterally (Rule G)
and affinally (Rule S), as listed in (19), in the same
fashion as the corresponding reference terminology.

(19) pārīˆyo   SPm(G,-S)   father-in-law
     pārīˆmo   SPf(G,-S)   mother-in-law
     jūaiˆyo   CSm(G,S-)   son-in-law
     jūaiˆco   CSf(G,S-)   daughter-in-law

The son-in-law and daughter-in-law terms are also
used to address all younger parallel cousins of the
sib and phratry, all children of sib brothers, and all
of the second descending generation of the phratry
outside of egoˆs lineage. However, they are not used
to address children of true siblings (cf. Goldman,
1963:134).

The second set is the same as the reference terms listed in (12) for siblings-in-law, except that the first two terms extend affinally (Rule -S) to same-sex co-siblings-in-law, namely, spouse's siblings' spouses.

Consanguineal precedence. Because of the prevalence of cross-cousin marriage and sister exchange, many Cubeos who are related to each other affinally were already related filially before their marriages took place. In every known instance, the kinship terms designating the closest filial relationship are used. For example, a certain boy's mother's sister married his father's father's brother. Before the marriage, he called the man grandfather (ʌjiñecũyo), but after the marriage he calls him parallel uncle (jipacʉmacʉ). Before the marriage, the boy's father called the kinsman parallel uncle (jipacʉmacʉ). After the marriage he could call him co-brother-in-law (ʌjitebucʉ), but he doesn't; he continues to use the consanguineal term, jipacʉmacʉ. By the same principle, after his marriage the kinsman calls the boy parallel nephew (ñʉjẽmacʉ,) rather than grandson (jipãrãmecʉ), but continues to call the boy's father ñʉjẽmacʉ.

We have seen that sibling terms are used for true and step siblings and parallel cousins and also for members of other sibs of the same phratry. The consanguineal relationship takes precedence over the sib relationship. For example, two sisters married men of different sibs of the same phratry; the elder sister married the man of the lower-ranking sib and the younger sister married the man of the higher-ranking sib. The younger sister's children call the elder sister's children `elder siblings'. If sib rank took precedence over relative age of true siblings, the younger sister's children would call the elder sister's children `younger siblings'.2

Conclusion

Primary importance is given to kinsmen of ego's own and adjacent generations, as is implied by a proliferation of terms in these areas, as opposed to just four grandkinsman terms for all other kinsmen beyond the first ascending and the first descending generations. Dravidian bifurcate categories of the Suruí type exhibit as a salient feature the consideration of the sex of all linking kinsmen, and not just those of the first ascending generation as in Iroquois systems, in order to distinguish parallel from cross relatives and thus identify potential spouses. On the basis of this preliminary study, further investigation can be done into the implications of the kinship system for social organization among the Cubeo.

NOTES

1
Two thousand or more Cubeos, whose language is Tucanoan, live along the Vaupés, Cuduyarí and Querarí Rivers and their tributaries. The data were collected from jejenawã, wadariwa, mia´dãwã, biowa, and codẽitarabuawu on those rivers as well as on the Piraboton. This investigation was carried out under the auspices of the Summer Institute of Linguistics during field trips undertaken from 1980 to 1983.

2The questions which this section on consanguineal precedence answers were raised by William R. Merrifield, the consultant under whom this paper was written. I am very grateful to him, not only for sharing his knowledge of kinship systems and their analysis, but also for his patience.

REFERENCES

Bontkes, Carolyn & William R. Merrifield. 1985. Suruí social organization. This volume.

Goldman, Irving. 1963. The Cubeo: Indians of the Northwest Amazon. Urbana: University of Illinois Press.

Lounsbury, Floyd G. 1964. The structural analysis of kinship semantics. In H. G. Lunt (ed.), Proceedings from the Ninth International Congress of Linguists, 1073-93. The Hague: Mouton and Co.

-----. 1965. Another view of The Trobriand kinship categories. In E. A. Hammel (ed.), Formal semantic analysis. American Anthropologist 67:5 (pt. 2):142-85.

Merrifield, William R. 1983. On the formal analysis of kinship terminologies. In F. Agard, G. Kelley, M. Makkai, and V. B. Makkai (eds.), Essays in honor of Charles F. Hockett (=Cornell Contributions to Linguistics 5), F. VanCoestsem and L. R. Waugh (gen. eds.). Leiden: E. J Brill. Pp. 371-404.

Salser, J. K. 1965-71. Unpublished field notes on Cubeo culture.

Salser, J. K. and Neva Salser. 1976. Fonología del cubeo. In Sistemas fonológicos de idiomas colombianos, tomo III, 71-79. Lomalinda: Instituto Lingüístico de Verano.

Waltz, Nathan and Carolyn Waltz. 1982. Notas sobre el parentesco guanano. In Linda L. Criswell (ed.), Artículos en lingüística y campos afines 11:1-27. Lomalinda: Instituto Lingüístico de Verano.

ON PAUMARI SOCIAL ORGANIZATION

Mary Ann Odmark & Rachel Landin
Summer Institute of Linguistics, Brazil

1

This paper presents patterns of residence, marriage, and kinship of the Paumarí people living in the Lake Marrahã area of Northwestern Brazil as of 1974. The Paumarí are seminomadic people living in close proximity to the dominant Portuguese-speaking culture. They have had contact with the Brazilians for over fifty years. They reside along the tributaries and lakes of the Purus River system.

SIL has had contact with the Lake Marrahã group since 1964. In the years that have followed, the Sepatini River group and several families from the Ituxi River group have joined with the Lake Marrahã group. There are still several families living on the Ituxi River system. Two men of the older generation disclaim relationship with some of the Ituxi River group. The younger generation claims relationships to all, probably because of more recent intermarriages. There are two uncontacted Paumarí groups. One is called `the unseen ones´ and is said to live on the Big Mamoriá River. The other group lives on some of the tributaries and lakes of the Tapoa River.

PAUMARI RESIDENCE

The Paumarí people living in the Lake Marrahã area tend to live in small groups comprising several nuclear families. They move between four main settlements. Figures 1 to 3 present the three settlements located on floodlands. Figure 4 presents the other settlement, located on high land. Floodlands are marginal, low areas of the river system which flood seasonally between January and May. High land is never inundated during the year. The majority of families have a house in more than one of these locations. A family may move to any of these places whether temporarily or for a longer length of time to engage in

93

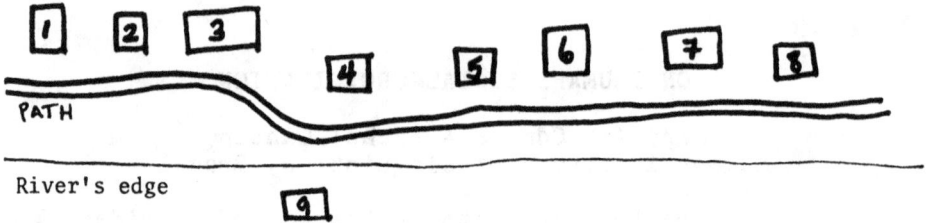

Figure 1. The Lake Marrahã floodlands village.

Figure 2. The Cacoria Beach (Purus
River) floodlands village.

Figure 3. The São José Beach (Purus
River) floodlands village.

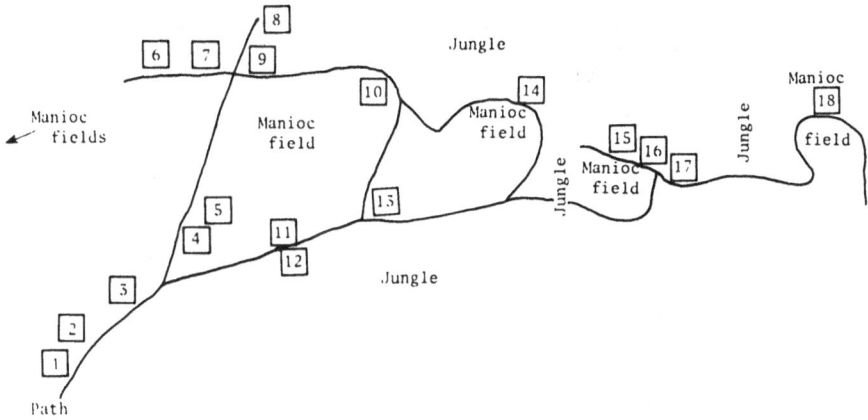

Figure 4. The highland village (near Lake Marrahã).

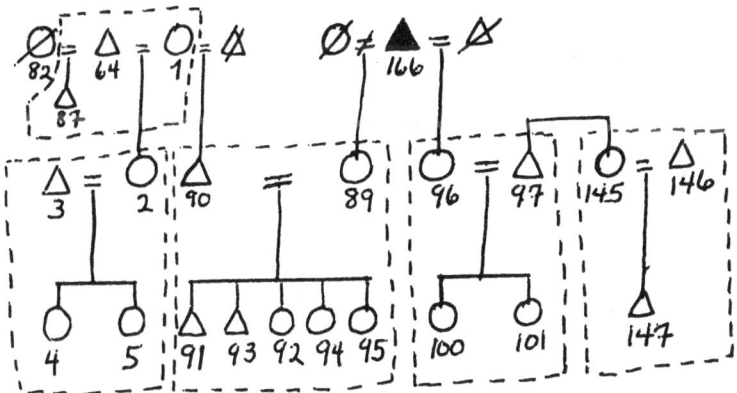

Figure 5. Occupants of the Lake Marrahã household 8.

shaded symbols – person not in residence

- family sleeping in a mosquito net

- house owner

activity for themselves or for some close relative who
has need of their labor. They plant their staple crop
of cassava and sweet potato root at two of the flood
land settlements and at high land. Some families make
a crop both on the floodlands and on high land.

When the Paumarí fish for themselves, the men
usually go after the big fish and the women and children go after smaller fish. The men usually take one
of the smaller children with them, preferably a male
child. Brothers go singly in their canoes to fish
together.

At high land where many have made their fields,
those who do not have fields may usually visit at the
invitation of someone who wants them to help in their
gardens. As payment, a helper receives a share of the
harvested product. There is much suspicion of those
who visit their extended families, because of a ten-
dency to steal from those who are not of the extended
family.

A single nuclear family may live temporarily in
locations other than the main settlements. They may be
accompanied by the brother's family to do work for a
Brazilian boss (patrão). Their work for him may
include such activities as fishing, rubber cutting,
gathering and breaking Brazil nuts, or cutting sorva.

Types of housing

The permanent type of housing is a wall-less structure built on stilts. These structures last about two
years and are built on both floodlands and high land.
The builder of a house is its owner. If a house is
temporarily vacated, however, another family may move
in and the returning owner may have to look for lodg-
ing elsewhere if the house is occupied by another
man's extended family.

Each nuclear family sleeps in a mosquito net on a
woven mat on the floor. An average of two to three
mosquito nets fit into the houses. Figure 5 presents
the occupants of one household with their kinship
relationships and sleeping arrangement.

If a house should be empty for any length of
time, the flooring, roofing, or even the main poles
may be taken by another person who is building himself

a house in that area. Nobody seems to get angry over this practice. Articles apparently abandoned or things not in apparent use can be claimed by someone else and this is not considered stealing.

Temporary constructions are made on beaches on floodlands. These are made with curved sticks stuck into the sand. Then woven mats made of palm leaves are thrown over the sticks for covering. If a family is traveling for more than a day, they tie a similar structure to the edges of their canoes.

At one lowland village, one nuclear family lives over the water in a rafthouse. Historically, the Paumarí lived on such rafthouses during high water and in little shelters on beaches during low water (Métraux 1948).

Constitution of a household

A household may consist of one nuclear family or a nuclear family and its extensions. The extended family can consist of a man, his wife, their children, their children's spouses, and grandchildren. It can also include any children of either the man or his wife by previous marriages.

Where several families live together, the older of the two couples is considered the head of the household. Generally, widowed old people past child bearing age are not considered heads of households, but are dealt with as with children.

True brothers do not generally live in the same household after marriage, though they tend to build houses next door to each other. An adult unmarried brother usually lives with his brother's family. The brother's wives do not object, as the children consider him as another father, and he provides fish for the household.

It is more common for full or half sisters and their families to stay in the same household. An example of this is found in households 16 and 17 (Figure 4). When the owner of house 16 is in residence, the family listed in house 16 moves into house 17. The two women, Sioniro (89) and Rasi (96), are half sisters whose mother is deceased (Figure 5). The father of Sioniro is Benjamin (166) who owns house 15.

The wife of the owner of 16 is Khoro (65). Her father is also Benjamin, and so she is half sister to Sioniro as well.

Female siblings also tend to have their homes built near their male siblings. A married sister may stay in the same house with her brother's family. Two examples of this are found in household 8 (Figure 1).

Ezilda (2) is the half sister of house-owner Babaji (90). Although Ezilda and her husband Ba?da?di (3) own house 4 in this village, it was occupied by another family. They preferred to stay with her brother rather than stay with Ba?da?di's half sister Bići (79) who lives in house 6. It is difficult to judge whether this is a preferred pattern or whether it happened because of the amount of housing available.

Kaboka (145) is Katena's (97) full sister. Kaboka and her husband Raimundo (146) and their child (147) were able to move in because of her connection to Katena even though Katena's right to stay in the house was through his wife Rasi, the sister of Babaji's wife.

Young children with only one living parent usually live with this parent. If the parent remarries and the child is not welcome in the new household, it is cared for by a relative. Kamaboa is a word used for 'orphaned' children with no living parents, with one living parent, or with two living parents where one of the parents has left the family to marry someone else. Kamaboa children are provided for in this way. Tonia (86) is an illustration. Her mother (82) had died. The father (66) remarried, and Tonia's two older brothers and sister are accepted by their father's new household. Tonia has not been accepted so she is being taken care of by Bií (79) who is her maternal parallel cousin.

A widowed old man who cannot remarry lives with his real child's family or with the family of a child he has raised. If he cannot attach himself to anyone in the community, he finds a Brazilian to work for who might supply his needs. Kavasiki (171) is an example. He lived with his widowed daughter Masí (102) who had several children, one of whom was a married son. As long as Kavasiki was contributing fish and food for them to eat he was accepted, but when he started

becoming senile, his daughter showed her displeasure
with his behavior. He then went to work for a Brazilian man who kept him until he became sick. He then
went back to the community and died without receiving
medical treatment.

Widows with children, without direct lineal relatives and who do not wish to remarry, can contract
with a collateral relative of a descending generation
to help provide food and other items for his household. An example of this is Raofanaro (155) who worked
for her cross nephew Honorio (20). He sustained her
while she helped his wife when his wife was in poor
health.

Marriage and residence

When a couple marries, they stay with the wife's
parents for the first month. Then they move to the
husband's parents' place of residence for a month.
They continue this residence exchange pattern for
about two years until they start having children. Then
they stay with each set of parents for a week at a
time. After they have two or three children they tend
to settle down and build their own house.

If the husband's parents are dead, a couple
usually stays with the wife's parents. If the wife's
parents are dead and she has true siblings, the couple
moves between the husband's parents and her siblings.
When both sets of parents are dead, the couple lives
with the wife's siblings for awhile and then moves in
with the husband's siblings for awhile as well. The
couple does not necessarily live in the same house
with their extended family but might build adjacent to
them.

Puberty festivals and residence

The entire Paumarí language community comes together as a whole to attend puberty festivals. They do
not stay in their regular houses but congregate in a
shelter using the ground as the floor. Two or three
days are spent for this occasion and if there is not
enough room for each family unit to hang their mosquito nets along the sides of the festival house at
night for the children to sleep in, some may build
temporary shelters with a shallow platform to keep
them off the ground.

PAUMARI MARRIAGE

Marriage among the Paumarí is preferred with a distant cross-cousin. It has been difficult to reconstruct genealogical links between spouses due to decimation of the group, but among fifty-one marriages studied, twenty-eight were between kinsmen of this category. In none of these marriages, however, were the cross cousins closely related.

Of the other twenty-three marriages, one man is married to his classificatory grandchild, five marriages were between a classificatory father's brother and his brother's daughter; four marriages were between a mother's brother and his sister's daughter; in twelve marriages, the spouses were in the parallel cousin category; and in one marriage the relationship was not documented.

A man may contract with a prospective father-in-law for his daughter. He usually lives and works for the prospective father-in-law before the marriage is consummated.

There are five Paumarí women married to Brazilian nationals. Of the five men, three are living with their wives and children in the community. One woman is married to an Apurinã man. She and her two children live in an Apurinã settlement. These six marriages to outsiders are fairly stable. From time to time other women have had Brazilian husbands for a short while, but in the end have settled down with Paumarí husbands. One Paumarí has married a Brazilian woman and they live in a Brazilian settlement.

Polygyny is not generally practiced. There is one man in the Ituxi River area who has three wives, two of whom are a mother and her daughter.

Out of fifty-one marriages during a ten year span, twenty-seven are still in existence and twenty-one have terminated. Of these twenty-one, six were terminated by the death of one of the spouses, the other fifteen for other reasons. Of these fifteen, nine marriages involved children and six marriages did not.

During the ten year period there were nine remarriages and seven first time marriages.

PAUMARI KINSHIP

Terms of reference

Grandkinsman terms. The three grandkinsman terms
are listed in (1). Terms in parentheses here and
elsewhere are those used in direct address.

(1) ?arahoda (badori)   PPm(1)^2 grandfather
     ?arahoni (mado)   PPf(1)   grandmother
     hanodi   CC(1)   grandchild

A single grandfather term classes together both
lineal male kinsmen of the second ascending generation. This term is also extended lineally and collaterally (Rule 1) to include all male kinsmen of more
than one generation above ego. A second term denotes
grandmothers in a corresponding fashion, merging the
two lineal grandmothers with female kinsmen two or
more generations above ego. A third term for grandchild is the reciprocal of the two grandparent terms.
It denotes the lineal descendants of ego of the second
descending generation, and extends to all kinsmen more
than one generation below ego--lineal and collateral
(Rule 1).

The extension of grandparent terms has been documented for up to the third ascending generation and of
the grandchild term to the second-descending generation descendants of ego's `siblings' and `cousins' and
to the children of ego's third descending generation
lineal descendants.

Parent and child terms. Two parent terms distinguish father and mother while one term reciprocally
denotes a child. The parent terms do not extend beyond
their primary senses. The child term may extend into
the second descending generation of ego's lineal descendants, especially if a child had been reared by
grandparents; but this may better be considered as
adoption rather than extension of the term, and probably works reciprocally with parent terms as well. The
parent and child terms are listed in (2). (A), in
parentheses, here and elsewhere indicates that the
reference term is used unchanged in direct address.

(2) abi?i (bi?i)   Pm   father
     amia (mia)   Pf   mother
     isai (A)   C   child

Collateral parent and child terms. Father's brother and mother's sister are distinguished from parents by two terms which extend to all corresponding male and female parallel kinsmen of the first ascending generation (Rule G), while two terms reciprocally mark the sex of the child of ego's same-sex sibling, as indicated in (3).

(3) badia   =PPCm(G)   father's brother
     madinava   =PPCf(G)   mother's sister
     badava   =PCCm(G)   same-sex sibling's son
     badnava   =PCCf(G)   same-sex sibling's daughter

The spouse of a parent, who is not himself or herself a parent of ego, is classified as a collateral parent by an equation which can be specified as the Step Kinsman Rule (4).

(4) PS --> =PPC

Stepchildren are referred to by descriptive phrases. A husband's child is called anamadinavahi, based on madinava `mother's sister'; a wife's child is called anabadiahi, based on badia `father's brother'.

Cross-kinsman parent and child terms. A third class of kinsmen of one generation distance is defined by another set of four terms, presented in (5).

(5) koko (A)   xPPCm(G)   uncle
     ?aaso (A)   xPPCf(G)   aunt
     bihadi (A, vido)   xmPCC(G)   nuncle
     makhononi   xfPCC(G)   naunt

The first two terms of (5) denote the mother's brother and the father's sister, respectively, and extend to all male and female cross kinsmen of the first ascending generation (Rule G). The second pair of terms are paired with the first two as their perfect reciprocals, designating cross kinsmen of the first descending generation and marking the sex of ego--the senior member of the ego/alter dyad--rather than of alter. Although bihadi is used in address, a second term (vido) is also used. Persons of the bihadi class are also often addressed by name.

Siblings. There are four sibling terms. Three terms mark relative age. Of these three terms, two designate sex. There is also a generic term for any

sibling, irrespective of age or sex. Siblings contrast
with cousins as parallel kinsmen, and all four sibling
terms extend to parallel kinsmen of ego's generation
(Rule G), as indicated in (6).

(6) ?aajo (A)   =ePCm(G)   elder brother
     adia (ba?ai)   =ePCf(G)   elder sister
     kajo?o   =yPC(G)   younger sibling
     igami   =PC(G)   sibling

Cousin terms. Cross cousins are classified by two
terms designating their sex. In their primary sense
the terms denote a kinsman related to ego through
ego's own parent and an opposite-sex, true sibling of
that parent. They extend to all cross kinsmen of ego's
generation (Rule G), as indicated in (7).

(7) javi (A)   xPPCCm(G)   male cousin
     ?ijimaro (A,?amo?amo) xPPCCf(G)   female cousin

Bifurcate categories

The concepts `parallel' and `cross', upon which
the above statements are made are of the Mayoruna type
(Fields and Merrifield 1977) which may be defined as
in (8).

(8) PARALLEL (MAYORUNA): Within the genealogical
     chain that links ego to a designated kinsman,
     there are an even number (0,2,4,...,n) of male
     kinsmen and an even number of female kinsmen.

     CROSS (MAYORUNA): Within the genealogical chain
     that links ego to a designated kinsman, there are
     an odd number (1,3,5,...,n) of male kinsmen and
     an odd number of female kinsmen.

Although Paumarí bifurcate categories are generally defined as of the Mayoruna type by the statements
of (8), Paumarí is more like Seneca (Lounsbury 1964)
than Mayoruna in the way it counts ego and alter in
respect to the definitions. In Paumarí, the sex of ego
is counted only in the classification of a kinsman of
the first descending generation; and, conversely, the
sex of alter is counted only when he or she is a first
ascending generation kinsman. Paumarí parallel and
cross dyads of ego's generation and of one generation
distance from ego are presented graphically in (9).

(9)
```
            *       *       *       *           *       *       *       *
            |\      |\      |\      |\          |\      |\      |\      |\
     *      m m     f f     f m     m f    *    m m     f f     f m     m f
     |\     | |     | |     | |     | |    |\   | |     | |     | |     | |
 m   m m    m m     m m     f m     f m    f m  f m     f m     m m     m m
 |   |      |       |       |       |      |    |       |       |       |
 *   *      *       *       *       *      *    *       *       *       *
 =   =      =       =       =       =      X    X       X       X       X

            *       *       *       *           *       *       *       *
            |\      |\      |\      |\          |\      |\      |\      |\
     *      m m     f f     f m     m f    *    m m     f f     f m     m f
     |\     | |     | |     | |     | |    |\   | |     | |     | |     | |
 f   f f    f f     f f     m f     m f    m f  m f     m f     f f     f f
 |   |      |       |       |       |      |    |       |       |       |
 *   *      *       *       *       *      *    *       *       *       *
 =   =      =       =       =       =      X    X       X       X       X

            *       *       *       *           *       *       *       *
            |\      |\      |\      |\          |\      |\      |\      |\
     *      m m     f f     f m     m f    *    m m     f f     f m     m f
     |\     | |     | |     | |     | |    |\   | |     | |     | |     | |
 m   m m    m m     m m     f m     f m    f m  f m     f m     m m     m m
 |\  | |    | |     | |     | |     | |    | |  | |     | |     | |     | |
 * * * *    * *     * *     * *     * *    * *  * *     * *     * *     * *
  =   =      =       =       =       =      X    X       X       X       X

            *       *       *       *           *       *       *       *
            |\      |\      |\      |\          |\      |\      |\      |\
     *      m m     f f     f m     m f    *    m m     f f     f m     m f
     |\     | |     | |     | |     | |    |\   | |     | |     | |     | |
 f   f f    f f     f f     m f     m f    m f  m f     m f     f f     f f
 |\  | |    | |     | |     | |     | |    | |  | |     | |     | |     | |
 * * * *    * *     * *     * *     * *    * *  * *     * *     * *     * *
  =   =      =       =       =       =      X    X       X       X       X
```

Terms of address

As indicated above, a number of terms of reference are also used in direct address, whereas other
terms have special vocative forms--in both cases the
vocative usage showing the same ranges over kintypes
as in reference use. There are, in addition, a few
cases where vocative usage differs systematically from
reference usage.

There is a single case, for example, of a class
of kinsmen, in reference, being divided into two
classes by vocative terms. Specifically, a single

grandchild term of reference classifies all junior
kinsmen more than a generation below ego, whereas two
vocative terms mark the sex of grandchildren, terms
which are not extended beyond their primary ranges, as
indicated in (10).

(10) makhini   CCm   grandson
     athoni   CCf   granddaughter

The remaining cases involve vocative terms which
merge classes of kinsmen which are distinguished from
one another by terms of reference. There are four such
terms.

First, parent terms of address are used both for
parallel, collateral kinsmen of the parent generation
as well as for kinsmen of the grandparent class, as
indicated in (11).

(11) papai   =Pm(G),PPm(1)   father
     mamai   =Pf(G),PPf(1)   mother

Secondly, two apparent synonyms are used to
address five classes of kinsmen (as defined by reference terminology): younger siblings, collateral sons
and daughters, naunts, and grandchildren, as indicated
in (12).

(12) xoni =yPC(G),=PCC(G),xfPCC(G),CC(1) jr. kinsman
     moxo =yPC(G),=PCC(G),xfPCC(G),CC(1) jr. kinsman

Many of the younger generation are being taught
from infancy to use Portuguese vocative terms to
address those of the first and second ascending generation as well as those of Ego's generation. The Portuguese terms they use are: vovô `grandfather´, vovó
`grandmother´, papai `father´, mamai `mother´, titio
`uncle´, titia `aunt´, mana `sibling´, primo `male
cousin´, and prima `female cousin´. Which terms of
this sort are used to address kinsmen of the first and
second descending generations is not known.

Five of the vocative terms occur with the possessive prefix `my´. They are isai `child´, makhini
`grandson´, athoni `granddaughter´, ?ijimaro `female
cousin´, and bihadi `nuncle´. Javi `male cousin´ may
be used with or without the `my´ prefix. The last
three terms are not widely used.

Affinal terms

Spouse terms. Two terms for husband and wife are presented in (13). They are common terms for man and woman, respectively. A wife often refers to her husband as `my child's father'.

(13) makiɓa   Sm   husband
     gamo   Sf   wife

There is a taboo that restricts husband and wife from addressing each other by name. It has been established in textual data that a husband may address his wife as ima?ihi `my old lady'. Among younger couples, Portuguese meu bem, an expression of endearment, is often used.

Parent- and child-in-law terms. Three affinal terms, as indicated in (14), match the three parent and child terms to denote the parents of spouse and the spouse of a child.

(14) hadi (koko)   SPm   father-in-law
     masodini (?aaso) SPf   mother-in-law
     aboni   CS   child-in-law

The use of aunt and uncle terms (koko, ?aaso) for addressing parents-in-law is a natural consequence of the practice of bilateral cross-cousin marriage.

Sibling-in-law terms. Four terms, listed in (15), denote siblings-in-law, marking both sex of ego and sex of alter. They are self-reciprocal in the sense of classing together spouse's sibling with sibling's spouse (Rule V). They also extend collaterally (Rule G) to all members of spouse's sibling class and to the spouses of all of ego's sibling class.

(15) vabo (ajabona) =mSPCm(V,G)   man's brother-in-law
     ?ananini   =fSPCf(V,G)   woman's sister-in-law
     makhidava   =fSPCm(V,G)   woman's brother-in-law
     anadiava   =mSPCf(V,G)   man's sister-in-law

Apart from ajabona, no other vocative terms have been discovered for siblings-in-law except for the use of Portuguese cunhado `brother-in-law' and cunhada `sister-in-law'.

Conceptual dimensions

In this section consanguineal kinship terms are described from the point of view of conceptual dimensions required to describe the systems of reference. The analysis focusses upon fully-extended senses of terms. The conceptual dimensions found to be most appropriate are as follows:

1. Genealogical distance, with the values:
    1.1 Ego's own generation.
    1.2 One generation distant.
    1.3 More than one generation distant.

2. Lineality, with the values:
    2.1 Lineal.
    2.1 Collateral.

3. Bifurcation, with the values:
    3.1 Parallel--within the genealogical chain that links ego to a designated kinsman, there are an even number $(0,2,4,...,n)$ of male kinsmen and an even number of female kinsmen.
    3.2 Cross--within the genealogical chain that links ego to a designated kinsman, there are an odd number $(1,3,5,...,n)$ of male kinsmen and an odd number of female kinsmen.

4. Seniority, with the values:
    4.1 Senior--older than ego if of his generation; otherwise, of an ascending generation.
    4.2 Junior--younger than ego if of his generation; otherwise, of a descending generation.

5. Sex of ego, with the values:
    4.1 Male.
    4.2 Female.

6. Sex of alter, with the values:
    5.1 Male.
    5.2 Female.

The terms of reference presented above are repeated in (16) with the addition of a conceptual definition in the form of a six digit number, each digit corresponding, in order, to the above six dimensions. Zero in a definition indicates that the corresponding dimension is irrelevant to the definition of the term.

As indicated in (16) and as the presentation of the terminology has reflected, there are three main classes of kinsmen, defined by genealogical distance, which may be termed grandkinsmen, familial kinsmen, and peers.

Lineality is a feature that only relates to familial kinsmen in that parent and child terms do not apparently extend beyond primary kintypes, although this distinction does not hold in direct address (Cf. 11).

(16)

?arahoda	PPm(1)	300101	grandfather
?arahoni	PPf(1)	300102	grandmother
hanodi	CC(1)	300100	grandchild

==

abi?i	Pm	210101	father
amia	Pf	210102	mother
isai	C	210200	child

----

badia	=PPCm(G)	221101	father's brother
madinava	=PPCf(G)	221102	mother's sister
badava	=PCCm(G)	221201	same-sex sibling's son
badnava	=PCCf(G)	221202	same-sex sibling's daughter

----

koko	xPPCm(G)	222101	uncle
?aaso	xPPCf(G)	222102	aunt
bihadi	xmPCC(G)	222210	nuncle
makhononi	xfPCC(G)	222220	naunt

==

?aajo	=ePCm(G)	101101	elder brother
adia	=ePCf(G)	101102	elder sister
kajo?o	=yPC(G)	101200	younger sibling

igami	=PC(G)	101000	sibling

----

javi	xPPCm(G)	102001	male cousin
?ijimaro	xPPCf(G)	102002	female cousin

Bifurcation has already been discussed as being of the Mayoruna type, a subtype of Dravidian which divides all but grandkinsmen into parallel and cross classes which, because of a strong preference for cross-cousin marriage, becomes a division between filial kinsmen and kinsmen-in-law.

Seniority is an important concept, being marked in all filial terms except those for cousins and the generic sibling term.

The role of sex in defining classes of kinsmen is complex and results in a certain amount of arbitrariness in trying to reduce the system to a conceptual statement. For most terms marked for sex, it is the sex of kinsman that is distinguished, but in almost all of these cases the kinsman whose sex is marked is also the senior member of the ego/alter dyad. For the cross familial kinsmen, however, it is clearly the sex of the senior member of the dyad that is marked. We have chosen sex of ego as the conceptual dimension, rather than sex of senior kinsman, on the strength of the fact that sex of ego is required for sibling-in-law terms. The conceptual dimensions of affinal terms are presented in (17). They presuppose an additional unmarked conceptual dimension which distinguishes kinsmen-in-law from filial kinsmen.

(17)
```
hadi       SPm           210101          father-in-law
masodini   SPf           210102          mother-in-law
aboni      CS            210200          child-in-law
===============================================================
vabo       =mSPCm(V,G)   101011      man's brother-in-law
?ananini   =fSPCf(V,G)   101022      woman's sister-in-law
makhidava  =fSPCm(V,G)   101021      woman's brother-in-law
anadiava   =mSPCf(V,G)   101012      man's sister-in-law
```

NOTES

[1]
Additional data for this paper were collected by MaryAnn Odmark in the Lake Marrahã settlement during July-November, 1974, and February, 1975, as part of a long-term field project begun in 1964 which is being carried out under contracts held between the Summer Institute of Linguistics, the Ministry of Interior, the National Indian Foundation (FUNAI) and the National Museum. The authors worked together on the analysis as part of a seminar held under the auspices of the Summer Institute of Linguistics in 1974 at Porto Velho, Rondônia, Brazil, under the direction of William R. Merrifield. Although various people were interviewed, the primary language consultant was Hiananiro, a widow of about 55 years of age.

[2]
Formal statements used in this article were first defined and illustrated for a long-delayed article (Merrifield 1983), but may also be seen in

Merrifield 1981 and Merrifield, Gregerson, & Ajamiseba 1983. Two rules of extension and one of inversion are required for Paumarí. The rules of extension are based on a general, filial extension rule which has the force of extending primary PC strings and which has two parts, as indicated in (18).

(18) THE FILIAL EXTENSION RULE: (A) $\emptyset$ --> P
                                                (B) $\emptyset$ --> C

> GENERATION EXTENSION (G): Apply parts A and B of the filial extension rule an equal number of times.

> EXTENSION RULE 1: Apply part A or B of the filial extension rule, or both, without limit except that, given a primary kintype of an ascending generation, B may apply only as many times as A; otherwise, if the primary kintype is not of an ascending generation, A may apply only as many times as B.

The inversion rule (V) moves S from one end of a PC string to the other, equating SPC (spouse's sibling) with PCS (sibling's spouse).

REFERENCES

Fields, Harriet L. & William R. Merrifield. 1980. Mayoruna (Panoan) kinship. Ethnology 19:1-28.

Lounsbury, Floyd G. 1964. The structural analysis of kinship semantics. In H. G. Lunt (ed.), Proceedings of the Ninth International Congress of Linguists, 1073-93.

Merrifield, William R. 1981. Proto Otomanguean kinship. International Museum of Cultures publication 11. Dallas.

-----. 1983. On the formal analysis of kinship terminologies. In F. Agard, G. Kelley, A. Makkai, and V. B. Makkai (eds.), Essays in honor of Charles F. Hockett. Cornell contributions to linguistics 5:371-405.

Merrifield, William R., Marilyn Gregerson, & Daniel C. Ajamiseba (eds.). 1983. Gods, heroes, kinsmen: ethnographic studies from Irian Jaya, Indonesia.

International Museum of Cultures publication 17. Dallas.

Métraux, Alfred. 1948. Tribes of the Jurua-Purus Basin. Handbook of South American Indians Volume 3.

KAYABI (TUPIAN) KINSHIP TERMINOLOGY

Helga Elisabeth Weiss
Summer Institute of Linguistics, Brazil

1

This paper is a modest contribution to our understanding of Tupian social organization by presenting an analysis of Kayabí kinship terms of reference and address. The paper is preliminary in nature, but provides a foundation for further research concerning the role kinship plays in Kayabí society.

Consanguineal terms of reference

Kayabí terms of kinship reference fall into three classes based on genealogical distance as defined by generation. The first of these three classes to be discussed is that of grandkinsmen.

Grandkinsmen. Grandkinsmen are kinsmen more than one generation distant from ego. The four grandkinsman terms are presented in (1).

(1)	ramɨy	PPm(1)	grandfather
	yarɨy	PPf(1)	grandmother
	remɨminũ	mCC(1)	man's grandchild
	remiarirũ	fCC(1)	woman's grandchild

The grandfather and grandmother terms denote lineal kinsmen of the second ascending generation, and extend both lineally and collaterally (Rule 1) to more distant kinsmen of two or more generations above that of ego.

The grandchild terms are perfect reciprocals of the grandparent terms, designating sex of ego but not of the grandchild. They designate persons of the second descending generation and beyond and all collateral kinsmen of those generations. Although Rule 1 theoretically extends indefinitely, given cross-cousin marriage and a very small population, genealogies do not in fact have great depth without developing close relationships through affinal alliances.

Parents and children. The second major class of Kayabí kinsmen, as defined by kinship terms, are kinsmen of the parent and child generations. This class is divided into two sets of kinsmen, parallel and cross. Terms for parallel kinsmen are presented in (2).

Two terms denote father and mother, respectively, and apparently have no extended senses in kinship reference. Two additional terms, the father and mother terms with the ending -?ɨt, denote the father's brother and the mother's sister, respectively, in their primary senses and extend collaterally to more distant nonlineal, parallel kinsmen of the first ascending generation. This has been documented to first cousins of parent and should be checked against further genealogical data to substantiate the likely case that the terms extend indefinitely.

(2)	rup	Pm	father
	ɨ	Pf	mother
	ru?wɨt	=PPCm(G)	father's brother
	ɨ?ɨt	=PPCf(G)	mother's sister
	ra?ɨt	=Cm(G),=fCf(G)	child
	ra?yɨt	=mCf(G)	man's daughter

In the first descending generation, two terms (both of which include the ending -?ɨt) range over lineal and collateral kinsmen in a complex way. The first term denotes both the junior male kinsman of ego of either sex and the junior female kinsman of a female ego; the second term denotes the junior female kinsman of a male ego. Two degrees of collateral extension of these terms (to the children of first cousins) have been documented.

The disjunctive definition of ra?ɨt may possibly be accounted for by a WOMAN'S DAUGHTER SKEWING RULE that equates a woman's female child with a male child, as in (3).

(3) WOMAN'S DAUGHTER SKEWING RULE: f --> m / .fC__.

The underlying meaning of ra?ɨt would then be considered to be Cm(G), with the skewing rule interpreting fCf as equivalent to fCm, a subset of Cm. The hypothesis needs to be tested against research into the role relationships of Kayabí parents and children as well as against comparative evidence from other, closely-related Tupian languages.

The second set of terms for kinsmen of one generation distance from ego consists of four terms for cross kinsmen, as indicated in (4).

(4) tutɨt   xPPCm(G)   uncle
     yaye   xPPCf(G)   aunt
     rekowiat   xmPCC(G)   nuncle
     peng   xfPCC(G)   naunt

Two terms denote the mother's brother and the father's sister, respectively, in their primary senses, and extend to all cross kinsmen of the first ascending generation. Two additional terms are perfect reciprocals of these, marking sex of ego rather than of alter.

Sibling and cousin terms. The third class of Kayabí kinsmen are ego's generation peers. There are seven terms, as presented in (5).

(5) reki?ɨt   =emPCm(G)   man's older brother
     rɨkiet   =efPCf(G)   woman's older sister
     rewiret   =ymPCm(G)   man's younger brother
     kɨpɨ?ɨt   =yfPCf(G)   woman's younger sister
     kɨwɨt   =fPCm(G)   woman's brother
     renɨt   =mPCf(G)   man's sister
     remi?uramet xPPCC(G)   cousin

As in the case of parent and child terms, kinsmen of ego's generation are divided into two broad classes, parallel and cross. Parallel kinsmen (siblings) are further classified by relative age, sex of ego, and sex of designated kinsman, which define six classes of siblings. Two reciprocal terms are used between older and younger male siblings, two others between older and younger female siblings, and two for siblings of the opposite sex without designating relative age--one term for a man's sister and its reciprocal for a woman's brother. All six sibling terms extend to parallel first cousins and, probably, beyond to other parallel collaterals of ego's generation (Rule G), but this last statement needs to be further documented.

Cross kinsmen (cousins) are all classified together under a single term, regardless of sex by a
single compound term which makes obvious reference to
a cross-cousin of the opposite sex of either side of
the family being a preferred marriage partner. Literally translated, the term means something like: thing-
eat-(future)-(perfective). The Kayabí verb `eat´ is
here used euphemistically of sexual intercourse.

Affinal terms of reference

There are only a few primitive terms of reference
for affinal kinsmen, most of them being composite
forms made up of a consanguineal term and a spouse
term. Though it is tempting to consider the composite
terms as mere descriptive phrases, there is evidence
that they are more than that. A consanguineal kinsman
is in some cases referred to by an affinal term subsequent to a marriage that relates him to ego in a new
way. Affinal terms may represent a recent innovation
that is only partially assimilated into the Kayabí
lexicon.

To denote the spouse of a consanguineal kinsman,
ego suffixes the combining form of a spouse term to
the consanguineal term which designates the kinsman.
The combining form for wife is -ratɨ, and for husband
is -wen. A few examples are: ra?yɨwen `man´s daugh-
ter´s husband´, rɨkiewen `woman´s older sister´s hus-
band´, tutɨratɨ `mother´s brother´s wife´, pengatɨ
`woman´s nephew´s wife´. As can be seen, certain
morphophonemic changes occur when the forms combine.

An unusual term, memɨtatɨ `woman´s son´s wife´,
includes a unique form for a woman´s child no longer
in use among the Kayabí. Lemos Barbosa (1967:88) lists
membyra as `woman´s son or daughter´ and membytaty as
`woman´s son´s wife´ for early Tupí.

Terms for spouse and for kinsmen of spouse are
presented in (6). The extension of the terms is not
well understood, and further analysis is needed. A few
observations may nevertheless be made.

Same-sex siblings of spouse are referred to by
composite terms made up of the regular spouse term
followed by the sibling term. Two unique terms are
used reciprocally by ego for spouse´s opposite-sex
sibling and for spouse of opposite-sex sibling. The

combining form of the wife term unexpectedly turns up
as the first element of the term for wife's father.
There is a unique primitive term for wife's mother and
also a reciprocal, which undoubtedly relate to the
special relationship of a Kayabí husband living in
matrilocal residence.

(6)			
	mən	Sm	husband
	remireko	Sf	wife
	menup	=fSPm(G,-S)	husband's father
	ratɨup	=mSPm(G,-S)	wife's fatner
	menɨ	=fSPf(G,-S)	husband's mother
	royo	=mSPf(G,-S)	wife's mother
	peum	=fCSm(G)	woman's daughter's husband
	meneki?ɨt	=efSPCm(G)	husband's older brother
	menewiret	=yfSPCm(G)	husband's younger brother
	remirekoɨkiet	=emSPCf(G)	wife's older sister
	remirekokɨpɨ?ɨt	=ymSPCf(G)	wife's younger sister
	raira?ɨt	=mSPCm(V,G)	man's brother-in-law
	uki?i	=fSPCf(V,G)	woman's sister-in-law

Terms for deceased kinsmen

Terms for a deceased consanguineal or affinal
kinsman are a combination of the reference term which
designates that kinsman plus the diminutive/endearment
ending -?i, with the exception of father and mother,
who are referred to by unique terms. These terms, like
those for living kinsmen, are preceded by an obliga-
tory possessive pronoun. Some examples are: ?ɨp
`deceased father', rɨrufət `deceased mother', ɨ?ɨ?ri
`deceased mother's sister', yaye?i `deceased father's
sister'. Names of deceased persons are never
mentioned.

Vocative terms

The Kayabí system for addressing consanguineal
and affinal kinsmen is extremely complex and will be
dealt with in a separate paper. Various sets of
vocative terms distinguish seniority, sex of ego and
alter, and respect. Choice of sets depend on types of
speech, such as greetings, address in conversation,
negative and positive statements, and other factors.

Componential analysis

A preliminary attempt at componential analysis of
the Kayabí reference terminology is presented in this

section. The early stage of analysis of vocative terms
precludes an analysis of any significance in this
area. Within the domain of kinship reference, the
terminology can be accounted for by a relatively
complex system of six conceptual dimensions. These
dimensions with their respective values are as
follows:

1. Genealogical distance, with the values:
    1.1 Kinsman is of ego's generation.
    1.2 Kinsman is one generation removed from ego.
    1.3 Kinsman is two or more generations removed
         from ego.
2. Bifurcation, with the values:
    2.1 Parallel--within the genealogical chain that
         links ego to the designated kinsman, the two
         kinsmen of the first ascending generation
         above that of ego or the kinsman, whichever
         of the latter is junior, are of the same
         sex.
    2.2 Cross--within the genealogical chain that
         links ego to the designated kinsman, the two
         kinsmen of the first ascending generation
         above that of ego or the kinsman, whichever
         of the latter is junior, are of the opposite
         sex.
3. Relative sex, with the values:
    3.1 Ego and the designated kinsman are of the
         same sex.
    3.2 Ego and the designated kinsman are of the
         opposite sex.
4. Seniority, with the values:
    4.1 Alter is ego's senior--older than ego if of
         ego's generation; otherwise, of an ascending
         generation.
    4.2 Alter is ego's junior--younger than ego if
         of ego's generation; otherwise, of a de-
         scending generation.
5. Lineality, with the values:
    5.1 Alter is a lineal kinsman of ego.
    5.2 Alter is a collateral kinsman of ego.
6. Sex with the values:
    6.1 Senior member of the ego/alter dyad is male.
    6.2 Senior member of the ego/alter dyad is
         female.
    6.3 Alter is male.
    6.4 Alter is female.

The conceptual definition for the extended range of each term of reference is indicated by a six-digit number in (7).

```
(7)   ramɨy       PPm(1)      300101                  grandfather
      yarɨy       PPf(1)      300102                  grandmother
      remɨminũ    mCC(1)      300201            man's grandchild
      remiarirũ   fCC(1)      300202          woman's grandchild
      =======================================================
      rup         Pm          210111                      father
      ɨ           Pf          210112                      mother
      ru?wɨt      =PPCm(G)    210121             father's brother
      ɨ?ɨt        =PPCf(G)    210122              mother's sister
      ra?ɨt       =Cm(G),=fCf(G) 210203,211204           child
      ra?yɨt      =mCf(G)     212204              man's daughter
      -------------------------------------------------------
      tutɨt       xPPCm(G)    220101                       uncle
      yaye        xPPCf(G)    220102                        aunt
      rekowiat    xmPCC(G)    220201                      nuncle
      peng        xfPCC(G)    220202                       naunt
      =======================================================
      reki?ɨt     =emPCm(G)   111101     man's older brother
      rɨkiet      =efPCf(G)   111102   woman's older sister
      rewiret     =ymPCm(G)   111201   man's younger brother
      kɨpɨ?ɨt     =yfPCf(G)   111202 woman's younger sister
      kɨwɨt       =fPCm(G)    112001        woman's brother
      renɨt       =mPCf(G)    112002            man's sister
      -------------------------------------------------------
      remi?uramet xPPCC(G)    120000                      cousin
```

The first dimension of genealogical distance defines three groups--members of ego's generation, members of generations adjacent to that of ego, and members of all more distant generations.

The second dimension, bifurcation is a significant dimension for all but grandkinsmen. The bifurcate categories are apparently of a standard Iroquoian type as found in Seneca (Merrifield 1983), but further study is required to verify this.

If this assumption (based on a minimum of data) is correct, the kinship dyads for up to two degrees of collateral distance are divided by bifurcate categories for kinsmen of one generation distance and for kinsmen of ego's generation as in (8).

The fourth dimension of seniority is quite important, having relevance to all but the cousin term, and

```
(8)                 *     *                 *     *
                   |\    |\               |\    |\
    *     *     * *   * *     *     *     * *   * *
   |\    |\    | |   | |    |\    |\    | |   | |
   m m   f f   m m   f f    f m   m f   f m   m f
   |     |     |     |      |     |     |     |
   *     *     *     *      *     *     *     *
   =     =     =     =      x     x     x     x

                    *     *                 *     *
                   |\    |\               |\    |\
    *     *     * *   * *     *     *     * *   * *
   |\    |\    | |   | |    |\    |\    | |   | |
   m m   f f   m m   f f    f m   m f   f m   m f
   | |   | |   | |   | |    | |   | |   | |   | |
   * *   * *   * *   * *    * *   * *   * *   * *
   =     =     =     =      x     x     x     x
```

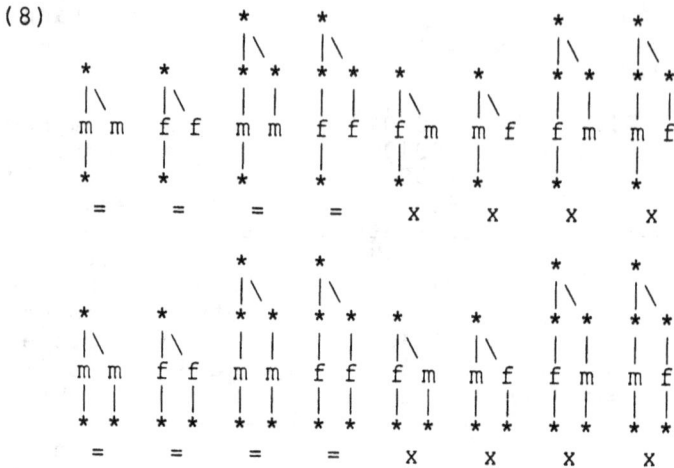

to two sibling terms where relative sex of ego and of kinsman is sufficient to set them off from the rest.

Dimension five, lineality, is only functional as a distinguishing feature between parents and their same-sex siblings.

Sex enters into the definition of kinsmen in dimensions three and six. Dimension three, the relative sex of ego and alter, is important in classifying parallel kinsmen of the child generation and of ego's own generation. Dimension six could be defined in any number of ways but is here considered to have four values. The first two values relating male and female to the senior member of the ego/alter dyad apply to terms for which dimension four, seniority, is diagnostic. In the case of terms for which seniority is not marked, the second two values relate male and female to the designated kinsman.

Although this system of analysis provides certain insights into the system, it does not provide a characterization of the system that is uniquely satisfying.

Summary

Limited genealogical data have permitted only a preliminary statement concerning Kayabí kinship terminology, but the pattern of kinship reference is fairly clear. Grandkinsmen encompass all kinsmen more than one generation from ego and are distinguished only by seniority and sex of the senior member of the ego/alter dyad.

Remaining kinsmen are classified as parallel or cross and as of ego's generation or one generation distance. Cross kinsmen of one generation distance are divided in the same fashion as grandkinsmen--by seniority and sex of the senior member of the dyad. All cross kinsmen of ego's generation are classified together. The concepts 'cross' and 'parallel' appear to be defined as for the Seneca (Iroquois).

Four terms distinguish parents from their same-sex siblings, while children--both lineal and collateral--are classed together with the exception of a man's female child. A second term designates this opposite-sex relationship.

Parallel kinsmen of ego's generation are defined by six terms--four which mark both seniority and sex for same-sex 'sibling' and two which mark the sex of opposite-sex 'siblings'.

More research needs to be done on vocative and affinal terminology, but affinal terms seem largely to be paraphrastic combinations involving consanguineal terms, possibly suggesting their relatively recent evolution as the result of cultural contact.

NOTES

[1] Kayabí has been classified as a Tupí-Guaraní language (Rodrigues 1958). The Kayabí are located on a Post of the Missão Anchieta on the Rio dos Peixes and in the Parque Nacional do Xingú. There are about 90 Kayabí at the Post and about 400 on the Xingú in Brazil. This paper is based on field work carried out among the Kayabí during the summer of 1974 as part of a longer study which began in 1966 in accordance with contracts held between the Summer Institute of Linguistics and the Ministry of the Interior, National Indian Foundation (FUNAI) and the National Museum, Rio de Janeiro. The writer wishes to thank William R. Merrifield for help furnished in the preparation of this paper during a workshop held in the Fall of 1974 at the Porto Velho study center of the Summer Institute of Linguistics. All Kayabí kinship terms of

reference must be possessed. They are presented in this paper as they occur with the pronoun ye- ´my´.

REFERENCES

Lemos Barbosa, Pe. A. 1967. Pequeno vocabulario Tupi-Português. Rio de Janeiro: Livraria São José.

Merrifield, William R. 1983. On the formal analysis of kinship terminologies. In Agard, Fred B., Gerald Kelley, Adam Makkai, and Valerie Becker Makkai (eds.), Essays in Honor of Charles F. Hockett, Cornell contributions to linguistics 5. Leiden: E. J. Brill. Pp. 371-404.

Rodrigues, Aryon D. 1958. Classification of Tupí-Guaraní. International Journal of American Linguistics 24:231-44.

www.ingramcontent.com/pod-product-compliance
Lightning Source LLC
Chambersburg PA
CBHW050535270326
41926CB00015B/3238